The Reverse Immigrant
Return to My Sicilian Roots

Alfred M. Zappalà
The Reverse Immigrant: Return to My Sicilian Roots
ISBN 188190750

Photo on cover courtesy of "Chi Ama la Sicilia Associazione di Promozione Sociale", Catania, Sicily.

For information and for orders, write to:

Legas

P.O. Box 149
Mineola, New York
11501, USA

3 Wood Aster Bay
Ottawa, Ontario
K2R 1D3 Canada

legaspublishing.com
Printed in Canada

Alfred M. Zappalà

The Reverse Immigrant

Return to My Sicilian Roots

LEGAS

Acknowledgements:

First and foremost, I'd like to thank the cast of characters that I mentioned in my essays, especially avv. Massimo Grimaldi of Catania. He is my best friend and brother.

I'd like to thank my mom and dad who instilled in me Sicilian pride. I'd like to thank my grandparents all four who immigrated to America in the early twentieth century. They were the original heroes. They are with God.

I'd like to thank my children Jennifer, Matthew and Catie who allowed me to take them to Sicily and see for themselves the joys and wonders of the Island.

I'd like to thank All Things Sicilian, a little company that a few of us started to show to America what Sicily is all about, and the nearly 5,000 email subscribers to my newsletter and readers of my blog www.allthingssicilian.blog.com.

I'd like to thank my friend and brothers in Sicily, especially Manfredi Barbera, Paolo Licata, Salvo Mammana, and all the other friends that Have there.

Mostly, I'd like to thank the twelve million Americans of Sicilian origin who hold the love of Sicily dear to their heart.

To Mom and Dad

"To have seen Italy without having seen Sicily is not to have seen Italy at all, for Sicily is the clue to everything."

Johann Wolfgang von Goethe

Contents

Introduction 11
    Chapter One 13
1. Basics 13
2. La Sicilia 15
3. At the Beginning 17
    Chapter Two: Old-timers 19
    Chapter Three: Is There a Mafia in Sicily? 21
    Chapter Four: The Old (Sicilian) Man 25
    Chapter Five: Ancients 27
1. The Battle of the Ancients 27
2. Ulysses Re-Visited 28
    Chapter Six: Healing Days 31
1. A Healing day 31
2. Springtime Inspection 32
    Chapter Seven: Humor 34
1. The Suave and Debonair American 34
2. The Electric Gate 35
3. My Little Putt-Putt 36
4. Sicilian Men 38
5. Rocking With Bonnie 39
6. The Key Tattoo…The Key! 42
7. Frutta and Polyester 43
8. The Sicilian Hot Dog 45
    Chapter Eight: Musings 48
1. Standing Our Ground Now and Forever 48
2. Re-Inventing Ourselves 50
3. Tough Times 52
4. Journey of Discovery 53
    Chapter Nine:
1. Massimo, Introduction 55
2. Cosi di pazzi 55
3. Lost in Translation! 57
3. The Banshee Kids 58
4. A Sicilian Shopping Spree! 59
5. Sicilian Baptism 61
6. Festa! Massimo's Birthday Party! 62
    Chapter Ten: Food in General 66
    Chapter Eleven: The New Place 68
1. Via Ulisse, No. 18. 68
2. Sure Beats Mickey D's! 68
3. Cleaning House…Sicilian Style! 70
4. It Isn't Exactly Heaven… 71

5. Day Four....Solitude 72
    Chapter Twelve: Holidays 75
1. The Legend(s) of San Valentino 75
2: Easter Essay 76
3. Sicilian Easter Traditions Essay Two 78
4. "Ferragosto" 79
5: A Sicilian Thanksgiving Story! 81
6. Christmas 82
7. On Christmas Again 83
8: Christmas Time Essay Three 84
9: Christmas Time Essay Four 85
10. Christmas Time Essay Five 86
11. Sicilian New Year's Feast 86
12. Nonno's Story 87
    Chapter Thirteen: Sunday Dinner 89
    Chapter Fourteen: Speaking Da Lingo! 91
    Chapter Fifteen: 92
1. Everyday Life 92
2. The Lido of the Ciclopi 93
3. You've Come a Long Way, Baby! 94
4. Whale Watching Sicilian Style. 95
5. Life by drive-through is purely American 97
    Chapter Sixteen: A VERY YOUNG MIND 99
    Chapter Seventeen 101
1. At The Market and Shopping 101
2. Sicilian Banshee Women! Shopping 103
    Chapter Eighteen: Seasons 105
1. Sicily in the Fall 105
2. Fireworks! It Must Be Summertime in Sicily! 105
3: The Sicilian Morning: November 106
    Chapter Nineteen: Secret Recipes 107
1. Legendary Killer Peppers 107
2. Yummy Summer Salad! 108
3. Feed Four For $15! 109
4. The Perfect Pasta 109
5. Alfred's Idiot-Proof Chicken Cutlets and Sauce. 110
    Chapter Twenty: Americani-Siciliani 112
1. Lou and Ceci 112
2. My Brother Tommy 113
3. Re-charging the Inner Soul 115
    Chapter Twenty-One: Sicilian Sunrise 118
    Chapter Twenty-Two 120
1. Ice Cream or Gelato? 120
2. Pupi Siciliani 121

Chapter Twenty-Three: Most Unusual People 123
1. Renzino Barbera 123
2. Joseph Privitera 124
3. Anna Privitera (Viagrande) 125
4. Leonardo Ciampa (Boston, MA.) 126
5. Mio Figlio Matthew 127
    Chapter Twenty-Four: 129
    Chapter Twenty-Five: 134
Driving: Introduction, Prelude and Aftermath 134
Introduction 134
Prelude 135
B: Aftermath 137
    Chapter Twenty-Six: Places 138
1. Road Trip! 138
2. Paradise on Earth: Nicolosi! 139
3. Trecastagni: A Healing day 140
4. Hey, Where's the Pepto-Bismol???? Castelbuono. 142
5. Cefalù: Another Hidden Jewel! 143
6. Mt. Etna....Aglow For the Holidays 144
7. Naxos 145
8. Capo San Vito 146
9. Mazara Del Vallo 148
10. Palermo: Brief History: 149
11. Santo Stefano di Camastra 150
12. Lu Triangulu di la Morti 152
13. Siracusa 153
14. Tindari 155
    Chapter Twenty-Seven 157
1. Prelude: Unity with the Soil. 157
2. Return to the Soil...after 85 years! 157
3. Aftermath: Visiting an old friend 159
    Chapter Twenty-eight: You'd Think I'd Learn! 161
    Chapter Twenty-Nine: Perpetual Rebirth 162
    Chapter Thirty: My Town 164
    164
1. Hither and Yon! 164
2. The Miracle in Lawrence 165
3. The Connection 168
    Chapter Thirty-One: Arrivals 170
1. Sicily....Blowing in the Wind! 170
2. Another arrival 171
3. Next Time I Will Swim There! 173
4. Holding My Breath 174
5. Leaving (or Coming) On A Jet Plane 175

Chapter Thirty Two: Departures 177
1. The Last Lamb Chop 177
2. Pre-Partum Depression and the Brioche 178
3. Same Old Thing 180
4. Big News! 180
5. Going Home...Or Leaving Home? 181
Chapter Thirty Three 184
Sant Agatha Patron of Catania 184
Chapter Thirty-Four: Going Native 186
1. Native in Two Days 186
2. Sicilian Doubting Thomas 188
Chapter Thirty-Five: Perfection 190
Chapter Thirty-Six 192
The Mighty Green Thumb 192
Chapter Thirty-Seven 194
Tripping the Light Fantastic 194
Chapter Thirty-Eight 197
Mom: A True Story 197

Introduction

.... On the sixth day.
God accomplished His work
And pleased with all the beauty
He had created
He took the earth in His hands
And kissed it.
There, where he put His lips,
That's Sicily
Renzino Barbera

Many people may think that I have finally fallen over the edge. Why? Well, what knucklehead would repeatedly board a plane and head to Sicily while its volcano is active, and then make plans to uproot himself from his cozy New England life and relocate to Sicily?

Why? Why not stay home and enjoy the May flowers in New England? Why not just go quietly into the sunset and visit La Sicilia every once in a while? Nope. Not me. My house in America is on the market and I plan on moving to Sicily as soon as humanly possible.

It wasn't always like this. Back in the 1990s, I was a law prof and a lawyer with a thriving law practice. When my dad died in 1996, I fulfilled a death bed promise to him that I would say a prayer for him at the Church of Sant'Alfio in Trecastagni, nestled on the slopes of Etna, which is our ancestral village.

When my feet hit the tarmac at Fontanarossa Airport in Catania a scant two weeks after I buried him, every molecule in my body screamed at me "Alfred, you are home."

I now feel like a fish on a beach in America. Trapped. Despite having made countless trips there since then, I am unfulfilled. No, I must reverse-immigrate. As my children tell me, "Dad, you belong there."

Yes, the economy is bad in Sicily; yes, the situation with the national debt may pull the EU apart, but what better location to be broke in than in Sicily? My condo in Acitrezza will be home. Maybe I will practice a little law there with my Italian partner, Massimo, focusing on import matters and dealing with Americans who need legal help in Italy. Maybe I will consult with Italian businesses that want to export items to the U.S. All I need to do is become fluent in Italian (not Sicilian) and I still have time to address that issue.

The Dalai Lama says, "The object of life is to be happy". I will now set a course to follow my dream. I am a dual citizen, so a visa is not an issue. I am a street kid from Lawrence, Massachusetts who learned how to survive, so why not? I can hop on a plane several times a year to see the kids and grandkids who can summer with their *Nonno* if they want (which they do and will).

So, why not? At my age can't I still follow a dream? My grandfather often told me, "We are all going to die someday" and I'd like to die in the shadow of Etna, in the place that courses through my veins. So, am I nuts? I don't believe so.

This little book contains a small portion of some of the adventures that I had: most humorous, some profound, all memorable. They are catalogued here in no particular order, as they are vignettes of my experiences there, the places I have gone, the people I have met, the feelings that I have experienced. This is one of those books that you can pick up anyplace and experience as adventures of the mind. I love Sicily. I hope you will too.

Chapter One

1. Basics

When I decided to write a book on Sicily, the first thing I decided NOT to do was write another travel book or a history book on Sicily. I wanted to share experiences that I have had there in a humorous or personal way.

I am an American. I was born and brought up in an American household and educated in American schools. My parents were first generation Americans making me a second generation American.

Sicilian, not Italian was spoken in my house. All four of my grandparents were Sicilian and immigrated to America in the early twentieth century. All came by "banana" boat, just like we see in the movies.

My grandfather Gaetano Torrisi was a homeless kid in Sicily taken in by a family in Trecastagni, near Mt. Etna. He later married one of the daughters. He came to America, found a job, sent for his wife, and had kids. A story that was repeated thousands of times in those days.

My other grandfather, Alfio Zappala came to America at that time too but never knew Gaetano in Sicily. He was a simple man, a hard working man.

Both started life in America working in the sweatshops of Lawrence, Massachusetts. My grandfather Gaetano later did what he did best, build things. He bootlegged, too. My grandfather Alfio just worked a hard worker's life like they all did in those days.

There is nothing original about their story. If you are of Sicilian ancestry, chances are you have a similar story.

However, it wasn't until I first visited Sicily in the nineties that I learned about the living conditions on the island, about its society, and about the reasons that compelled millions to leave and set a new life in America.

Almost every occupying nation sucked them dry. Almost every occupying nation oppressed, killed, drained away and exploited everything Sicilian. The sword, the rifle, the bomb all were the weapons of choice.

Sicilians have never had a chance to breathe. This is why they left in droves at the turn of the century. They left with hearts torn out of their bodies, their spirits oppressed.

Most Sicilians embraced the new life in America. America, not Sicily, was their home. Some families even forbade their kids from speaking Sicilian at home. Fortunately, mine did not.

Over the years, growing up in America and not knowing any other way of life, I assumed that being Sicilian was just like being Irish, German, French, Greek or any other nationality. I was wrong.

Being Sicilian is special. Very special.

Now, as I get older and have taken the time to research the true history of Sicily, I realize how little American-Sicilians know about the place.

Most have heard second or third or fourth hand stories from their parents, grandparents or relatives.

Unfortunately, some Sicilian- Americans have exploited her too and have become wealthy doing so. There is a long and continuing line of Mafia-like movies and television series that denigrate Sicily and Sicilians. So called beautiful "art films" have exploited my people in America. When is the last time you saw something on TV about Sicily that wasn't Mafia related?

Is there a Mafia in Sicily? Yes. Are they ruthless killers? Yes! Are they a disgrace? Yes!

But aren't there gangs and thugs in America, too? Yes. Far more. Newspapers now list gangs from all over operating with impunity in America.

Can you name two famous Sicilian composers? How about a single famous art master? Can you name one of the two popes that were Sicilian? How about a famous scientist, mathematician, writer, poet, intellectual?

Most Americans can't.

As a matter of fact, most Americans don't know the history of Italy very well either.

Hopefully, these writings will motivate the reader to do research on their ancestral home. Hopefully the light of love and pride will be turned on .There are twelve million Sicilian-Americans...double the current population of Sicily right now.

In this economic climate, young college graduates there are leaving in droves. There is a critical intellectual blood letting going on now that is heart breaking.

Sicily is still tangled in the caste system, too. It is not what you know, but rather who you know in Sicily, as it has been for thousands of years. Thus, we need to fix this.

I love Sicily and her treasures more than life, I think. I want her to be stable and prosperous. I want the whole world to appreciate her beauty, her culture and her people.

It may well be an impossible task, but I chose to join the ranks of those who care about her, and I bet you too will join those ranks after thinking about it a bit.

2. La Sicilia

Many who have never gone to Sicily often ask me where they should visit in Sicily.

That's like asking someone which side of a delicious cake do you start eating? The left, right, or middle? If I had to suggest just four areas to visit, they would be Palermo, Agrigento, Taormina, and because of ancestral bias, Catania.

Let me say first that seeing "only" four areas is vastly insufficient. If you are a Sicilian-American, a visit to your ancestral village or city trumps my list. After having traveled there over 40 times the last 15 years, and after having spent weeks there at a time, let me say that there are many other places just as charming, historical, and wondrous as the four areas that I am about to suggest that you visit!

My list:

Sicily is the world's first multicultural society. My Sicily was once a Greek colony, a Norman kingdom, a Roman province, an Arab emirate and a Spanish colony. The Phoenicians,Carthaginians the Swabians, Angevins, and Aragonese have all called Sicily home at one time or another and they've left behind an interesting and diverse history that is filled with mystique.

Thus, a great starting point for you is on the west side of the island: Palermo.

Palermo was founded as a port during the eighth century B.C. Today, it is the largest urban center in Sicily. Its Feast of Santa Rosalia draws hundreds of thousands yearly and is a wonder to behold.

Be sure to visit the city center and the wonderful convents, palaces, monasteries, and churches that make up the "old town." The city center is a blend of Arabic and Norman architecture and second to none in historical significance. Most of the outlying areas of Palermo were destroyed during the Second World War and dishonest men built many concrete apartment houses which cast blight on certain areas. However, there are seven theatres in the city center if you wish to spend a night on the town, one more beautiful than the other.

A must-see is the Royal Palace, a spectacular architectural structure that was built in the twelfth century. Other things you won't want to miss include the Cathedral and the Regional Archaeological Museum, which houses an extensive collection of Greek and Etruscan art.

Palermo is at the top of my list, for sure.

On Sicily's south coast, you will find Agrigento and the Valley of the Temples. Today, these ancient Greek ruins are a UNESCO World Heritage Site. There, you can visit the remains of the Greek city of Akragas, where the Doric temples were built in the fifth century B.C. The Museo Archeologico has a large collection of artifacts on display that include exquisite funerary urns and statues. At dusk, the area is surreal with the silhouettes of temples outlined against the night sky, as the sun gives way to the moon. Agrigento will captivate your soul.

On the East coast, no visit to Sicily can occur unless you visit Taormina. This "Pearl of Europe" is a mountain top village offering spectacular views of Mt. Etna, 200 meters above sea level, gazing down on the Ionian Sea. The town drips of history, art, scenery and culture that will take your breath away. You will be in wonderment as you walk the winding, medieval streets. Corso Umberto, Taormina's main street, cannot be adequately put in words.

Ice cream bars, cafes and restaurants can be found at every turn. The Wunderbar is my favorite. When you visit the Greek Theatre that was built in the 3rd century, you can see a magnificent view of Mount Etna. It's a wonder to behold and another experience you won't want to miss.

The second largest city in Sicily is the city of Catania, located on the southern coast. The city has survived its share of disasters, including heavy bombing during WWII, famines, epidemics, the eruption of Mount Etna in 1669, and in the past, hordes of marauding pirates. After the devastating eruption of Mount Etna, the city was completely rebuilt. Mount Etna plays an important role in the lives of the people of Catania. Homes, walls, buildings and roads are all built using black, volcanic rock.

Catania has two Roman amphitheatres. At one time over 14,000 spectators gathered in the largest to watch sporting events and to socialize. Each year Catania hosts the festival of Saint Agatha, the second largest festival in Sicily. For two days, a statue of Sant Agatha is carried in the "vara" by her believers.

Two of Italy's most famous artists, Vincenzo Bellini and Giovanni Verga, were natives of Catania. Both have museums dedicated to them: the Bellini Civic Museum and the Giovanni Verga House Museum. Catania is known for its restaurants, clubs and shops. It's a city that is full of sights and sounds that will fill you with awe and delight. The Fish Market is an interesting way to spend a morning, too.

Arancine, (rice balls), mussels, calamari, swordfish, prawns, and of course, pizza are some of my personal favorites in Catania. No visit to Catania can be complete without trying a delicious cannoli, gelato, granita or cassata. Remember: that diet can always start tomorrow!

3. At the Beginning

What is a Sicilian?

Sicilians are Greek, Roman, Arab, Norman, Austrian, Spanish, with English, African, and Phoenician thrown in for good measure just to scratch the surface. We are a massive blend of peoples, cultures and thought churned and created over nearly three millennia of conquest, oppression, and occupation. And the predominant quality of the Sicilin is tolerance for diversity. Maybe the folks in Iraq and Afghanistan can take a lesson. Maybe even the Palestinians and Israelis.

Each occupier left its mark. Each occupier left its tribute. The Greek ruins in Agrigento and Siracusa, the Roman villas at Piazza Armerina and ruins in Taormina, the Norman cathedrals of Monreale and Cefalù, Acicastello, the mosques and castles of Palermo and Catania, the Spanish mansions of Messina: all are the tip of the iceberg in understanding the essence of a Sicilian.

Today Palermo teems with exotic colors and textures…a throw back to the days of old.

Mazara Del Vallo, Marsala (the Port of Allah), and Sciacca still bear the Saracen influence.

The Greek Theaters in Taormina, Catania, and Siracusa testify to the ancients from the east.

Enna bears a striking Spanish influence, as anyone who has witnessed the Good Friday Procession of the faithful can testify. The Castello Di San Marco near Giardini bears witness to this also.

Blend the cultures together, add over two thousand years or so and presto, a Sicilian emerges!

Probably the most fought over piece of real estate in the European continent, her people over the centuries have experienced war, eruption ,earthquake, and always occupation.

Still, she persisted. And so her people.

Still she influences anyone who came and will come.

The magical allure of her beauty influenced Homer and countless artists, writers, musicians, poets and other talented people too numerous to mention.

Her people have achieved greatness all over the world.

She is singularly the biggest treasure in all of Europe, with Taormina, that Pearl of Europe, sitting as her crown jewel just a stone's throw from Mt. Etna, magical Mt. Etna, who gives and takes away.

Walk the street of Catania, destroyed three times by Etna's fury over the centuries, or sit on the beach to the south at Marina di Ragusa or feel the ancient Greeks at Agrigento, it's all the same. Every speck of my Island is alive and her breath refreshes my soul.

That, my friend, is the essence of Sicily, and of being Sicilian.

Chapter Two

Old-timers

I won't forget them, and neither will you. Old-timers.

They weren't always old. They were once strong and vibrant.

They are the members of the generation that immediately preceded me: the immigrant generation now in their eighties and nineties.

Most were simple folks. Most started their lives somewhere in Europe. Sicily, Ireland, Poland, Spain, Portugal, or Germany.

They or their parents came to America as a result of tragedy, poverty, necessity. Very few came because they wanted to. Truth be told, they came here to survive.

Now, they are dying off.

We buried my mom recently. It was a celebration of a long life. While members of my family wept and reminisced, we were happy that we had enjoyed her for so long.

As her friends stopped by to pay their respects—the surviving friends, that is, people that I infrequently see now—I pondered life and what it does to a person over time.

Life is like the never ending sea whose waves lap the shoreline. Over time the strength of the sea always wins, slowly dragging the sand of the beach back to whence it came.

As I saw these old timers, many with canes now, others assisted by younger loved ones, still others in wheel chairs, I reflected on their longevity and the life that they lived.

All of them experienced the Great Depression. All of them experienced World War II. Most of them were in their prime of life in tthe forties, fifties, and part of the sixties.

Survivors of another era they are.

They had no television, computers, IPODS, DVDs. They had no microwaves, refrigerators that made ice, air conditioners or sleek cars.

Heck, most started life in cramped apartments in a city: Lawrence, Boston, New York, Chicago, Philadelphia.

Almost all had no health insurance, unemployment or worker's compensation. There was no such thing as a 401-k retirement account. At most, a simple "pension" from one of the sweat shops.

They worked in terrible conditions. Most worked "piecemeal:" they got paid for what they did.

Almost all were bi-lingual latch key kids growing up, although those social terms had not yet been invented.

They amused themselves with simple parlor games.

They saved their money with "Christmas Clubs," scrimped their way thru life, and if they had anything saved, they gave it to their kids to help them pay for private elementary school, high school or college.

They were the generation of sacrifice.

Now, they are old and dying off every day. Their fragility caused by life and the passage of time.

I thank them. Each and every one of them. Both the departed and those still clinging to life.

They all are my heroes.

Chapter Three

Is There a Mafia in Sicily?

I have been asked a million times by people who know that I frequently travel to Sicily:

"Alfred, is there a Mafia in Sicily today?"

My answer has always been the same: "Sure."

In Italy it's called the Parliament and in the United States it's called Congress. If you mean "thugs" again the answer is the same: they are both here in the States and there, as well. Crime has no international boundaries.

You have to understand that Sicily has only 6 million people living there. The population of the whole island is smaller than New York City. Thus the problem there is magnified as there isn't as much going on otherwise, truth be told. America has twice as many Sicilians living here than there.

Italy was and is in an entirely different country from the USA. When Italy was devastated during the Second World War, an enormous power vacuum was created. Many cities were bombed out, and many Italians killed. Starvation was a way of life in 1943 until 1947, and that is when organized crime took root. Originally, it was a protection type of thing. It existed in the nineteenth century, but post WWII it really took root.

As time went on and its influence grew, aided by the Americans, things dramatically changed.

Organized crime in Sicily, which had been almost stamped out by Mussolini and his Fascists, fought against the Fascists and Nazi regimes under the Arab "An enemy of my enemy is my friend" theory. Thus, both Sicilian and American organized crime aided American forces in the invasion of Sicily and Italy. As a result, when the war ended, elements of organized crime were able to step into the power vacuum and take advantage of the situation.

For example, one Mafia leader who had helped the Americans was allowed to keep all the American army trucks that were abandoned or left behind. Overnight, a trucking company and bus company was created... run by the mob....and that company still exists today, although in a different form.

Some of the very biggest Italian companies can trace their roots in this manner. So could some in the Vatican, especially in Vatican banking practices. Corruption, influence, and power seeking was the norm.

We see it today in Iraq and Afghanistan as a matter of fact. Bodies have littered the country the last eight years as the Americans want to hand over control to them and leave....and people are killing for that opportunity. Is that about religion or wealth and power? The same thing happened in Sicily.

A brisk black market in military food, clothing and supplies after the war helped the criminal organizations in Sicily grow by giving them money to expand into different criminal enterprises, especially drug processing, with the "hub" being on Palermo. Thus, Americans unwittingly helped to create the menace that was came to be known as La Cosa Nostra.

With its insatiable appetite for drugs, from the fifties to the nineties, America's lust for heroin and cocaine fueled its expansion. As a rule, few Sicilians do drugs. To Sicilian criminals, drug processing, and drug transport was strictly an export crop.

Banks were set up to launder money in America, the Cayman Islands, England, and Switzerland. Billions flowed into their coffers every year and money bought power everywhere. Politicians, law enforcement, journalists all fell in line. Those who didn't were killed.

The bodies of important people that littered the streets of Palermo had a name: they were the "distinguished corpses", and there were many during this period. American organized crime, especially many of Sicilian origin, had helped the American military for the Sicilian invasion, and they prospered after the war too.

In many cases Sicilian ports had been sabotaged and railways damaged thru connections developed with the American and Sicilian organized crime gangs in preparation for the invasion and pay back was in order.

In addition, 15% of the invading American forces were Italian-Americans. Some of them became involved in criminal enterprises: one of the first criminals in Palermo after the war was actually an American colonel who stayed there!

Thus, the real problem started after the war when the Americans handed over power to these criminal elements that had helped them. They now controlled just about everything, and it was a matter of time before different elements began to fight over the opportunities.

The foxes were put in charge of the chicken coops. Remember, there was no one else.

The Sicilian Mafia filled a void, and between 1946 and 1984 the streets were filled with blood, especially in Palermo, as the First and then the Second Mafia War were fought by criminals vying for control. The gangs of Corleone, the most brutal and deadly of all, ultimately conquered, eliminating the criminals from Palermo.

During this period, things were very bad in Sicily (and all of Europe for that matter), and the reputation of the Mafia grew.

Politically, Italy during this period was recovering from the war. Governments fell every single year. Because the Sicilian Mafia could deliver votes for the entire island, their power grew with those in power, and with those who wanted power, especially the Christian Democratic Party. Political intrigue was the order of the day.

Thus, there were two governments in Italy post-World War: The Italian government and the Sicilian Mafia, connected with many links at the very highest level, including the office of the Prime Minister!

It wasn't until the assassination of two anti-mafia magistrates, Judges Falcone and Borsellino that the population raised in revolt against organized crime. Thousands of criminals were denounced and then some began to talk: they are known as the "penitents". Finally, the vow of silence had been broken. As prosecutions increased over the years and more and more criminals turned state's evidence, a grim picture of corruption, murder, money, power, drugs, money laundering, and much more emerged.

To this day, the fight continues, but the most dangerous have long been jailed and with joint American, Italian and European efforts, the menace seems to be fading, although it's not eliminated entirely, for sure.

An enlightening experience for those interested in the origins of the Mafia in Sicily is to start by doing a search on Wikipedia and review this tumultuous era.

A remarkable book by journalist Peter Robb, who lived in Sicily for fourteen years, called *Midnight in Sicily* recently rose to the *New York Times'* best seller list and cast a light on this dark period of Sicilian history. I recommend it as a terrific snapshot of a terrible era.

It wasn't until the 1990s that the Italian government finally "matured" enough to take on the Mafia, especially after the assassination of Falcone and Borsellino.

Thus, the fight is less than twenty years old, and continues to this day. Recently, the son of one of the capos of that era was arrested in Brazil. It made all the headlines in Europe.

Today, most of the leaders of that era are in jail for life, and the Italian anti-Mafia forces continue to pursue the remnants.

It is said that the Sicilian Mafia's economy was as big as or bigger than the Italian economy in its heyday, and that international banking was very much at fault too. The two biggest bank failures in America, as a matter of facts, were directly tied to the Mafia, as was the fall of the Vatican Bank.

In time, articles about the Mafia will fade from the headlines as Sicily further develops. If good jobs were available there, potential criminals would perhaps lead a different life. Then again, isn't the same true here? If young city kids had jobs and a better way of life, would youth gangs be so large and dangerous today here in America?

For the "average" person, the Mafia is only an idea developed by movies like *The Godfather*. It was romanticized. Very nice music was played in the background as people were killed on film.

Today, a different Sicily exists. A beautiful, historical, wondrous land full of wonderful people who struggle every day to live, just like you and me. Their struggle, however, is two thousand years old. Ours isn't.

Sicily cannot hide from its past, nor should it.

Lessons need to be learned. Sicilians should adopt the motto: "never forget"

Then again, there are skeletons in every country's closet. The Holocaust in Germany, the French Revolution, The rape of South and Central America by the Spanish, the genocide in Cambodia in the seventies, Rwanda in the nineties…Darfur today….the list is endless, it seems.

America can be included too: slavery, the American Indians. Mankind must learn from these catastrophes, and always keep the lessons before their eyes.

Darwin says our species evolves.

I sure hope he evolves into a better human being.

Chapter Four

The Old (Sicilian) Man

On a windy and rain-swept day, this morning I went to Acitrezza.

I feel the spirit of the ancient Greeks and Romans there. I see the Greek ships from two thousand years ago as they approach the rocky shoreline and imagine how many of them were hurled to their demise against the unforgiving rocks.

Really, in this beautiful place, I bet there is a lot of sorrow too.

The people of this village have seen it all through the centuries, this I know.

Tourism in the summer, desolation in the winter. The whole gambit of things, I think.

God, what a beautiful place. A metaphor of Sicily: black and white. Good and evil. Beauty and ugliness. The good and the bad. Bountiful harvest and famine. Everything has happened here through the millennia.

Today, it is deserted. I have it all to myself.

The rocks of the Cyclopes, which according to the legend were hurled by Poliphemus at Ulysses after Ulysses blinded him, jut out of the water and loom large in the bay.

Shops and pizzerias now shuttered for the winter line the street opposite the water.

Only the small fish shops are open, selling this morning's catch to the locals.

I wander around and smell the sea. Mystical.

From the deck of my new condo, with its panoramic view second to none in all of Sicily, this morning as I had my coffee, I looked out below and saw the tiny boats of the fishermen fight the sea's rage with many struggling to remain afloat.

I worried for them. For sure, I thought, someone would get hurt today.

That is why I went down to the water's edge. I wanted to feel the power of the waves.

Interestingly, I bumped into a man who was tending his small shrimp skiff. The boat was no more that 15 feet long. He had that weathered look…that Old Man of the Sea look. Tough eyes that had seen everything in life, I guess. Wearing a thick sweater, a slicker jacket and a cap pulled over one eye. I wished I had brought my camera to capture the moment.

We talked. In my halting Sicilian, I asked if he has fished in the morning. He had. The tide had pulled the shrimp and squid close by, he said, so the catch was plentiful.

I asked about the waves. Wasn't he afraid?

"U mari prima duna e poi pigghia!"

"The sea," he said "first gives and then takes."

Today it gave. Someday, but not today, it will take.

I continued down the street.

That fisherman is very special, I think.

Braver than me, for sure.

Chapter Five

Ancients (2010)

1. The Battle of the Ancients

The crack from the angry sky startled me. In a matter of minutes, the sky had turned from a hazy blue to an ominous black. Just like that. The rain began to pound and then the lights went out. Thank God for the battery on the laptop. Being the dolt that I am, I quickly unpacked the bags that I had carried into the house. I had just returned from Le Zagare in San Giovanni La Punta where I bought some new stuff for the kitchen (glasses, cups, dish drainer, and a bunch of cleaning supplies for the guy who cleans my house when I leave next week). For twenty euros, I bought a lot of stuff today because of the big sale that I had read about. Everything was 45% off. Hurrying to put stuff away, I was going back out in the terrible weather to a special place I go to when the weather is like that. I always go here. My spirit is connected to this beautiful yet terrible place. At least my car, which until twenty minutes ago was filthy with volcanic ash that accumulates every once in a while when Etna spews, would be cleaned. I pushed the empty Windex bottles aside (here I travel with Windex and old rags…the windows are always filthy) and hopped into my chariot. Down the winding roads of Acitrezza I went. The roads were almost flooded with rivers of water cascading down the hills. I turned my wipers up to maximum and even put on my seat belt, something I never do.

I drove thru the downpour. Sicilians hate rain. They think they are going to melt. The roads were deserted and it was mid afternoon. Hitting a huge puddle, I wasn't going to be denied today. Driving thru the village I saw the fishermen unloading their catch, boats tied to their moorings. I drove on.

Finding my destination, I parked my car. Thank God I keep my all weather gear here. My rain slick was the perfect protection today. I had purchased it a few years back when I lived in Amsterdam, and this coat and I had been thru plenty of tough Dutch weather. It was ready today for me after hanging in my closet for many months. The sky cracked again. Black clouds and now the wind howling. Jesus, it was bad.

I arrived at my destination: the Norman Castle in Acicastello. Here, on the mouth of a huge bay, stood the ancient castle. They call it the Norman castle because the Normans in the 11th century were the last to modify it, but this place had been a Saracen castle, a Roman fortification and before that, a Greek fortification. Old. Very very old. Sacred ground. The place is sacred because a river of blood has been spilled over this location. Whoever controlled Acicastello, controlled the shipping routes north and south. Probably the most strategic location from Catania to Siracusa. In any case, I was here. Rain driving against my face, I gazed into the Bay. The waves were furious. The surf pounded the castle. Today, in my mind, at this spot, I relived the battle between the ancient Roman Caesar Augustus (Augustus) and the son of Pompey, Sextus Pompey. This battle took place over two thousand years ago. Sextus Pompey, after his father's death, fled to Sicily with his fleet and began to intercept the grain shipments from Egypt heading to Rome. As a result, Rome was starving, and Augustus was here to defeat Sextus. All day and night the enormous battle raged. Grappling hooks bound the ancient war ships together and deadly hand to hand combat took place. Thousands of corpses floated on the bay after the fierce battle.

Today, I saw it all. I relived the battle, which took place in fierce weather. I heard the screams, the battle cries. I saw the legionnaires in battle gear. I even saw Augustus in his Consul ship. The fleet of Sextus was all Roman, too. Thus this battle pitted Roman against Roman. My heart pounded, my soul grieved for the ancient dead. Augustus eventually defeated Sextus and had him beheaded. Thus was the start of the Pax Romana, and Augustus ruled for the next forty years as Rome expanded her empire to include Egypt, Iran, Iraq, Turkey, Palestine and the whole Mediterranean region. The decisive battle was here, and I witnessed it. Today.

When I am home and it rains, I usually stay inside and watch the tube. Today, in my mind, I watched history. Again.

PS: Acicastello also was the place where the Greeks of Siracusa defeated the ancient Carthaginians 1000 years before this battle. A long, long time ago. God, I love this place.

2. Ulysses Re-Visited (2009)

In Homer's *Odyssey*, Ulysses was blown off course after he helped sack Troy. He was on his way home when a huge storm blew him off course. For ten years, he wandered the Mediterranean.

Homer wrote that the Mediterranean's fury often came suddenly, calm waters suddenly turning vicious with crashing waves and howling wind.

It was appropriate that I witnessed such a thing yesterday, especially in Acitrezza, where Ulysses and his band of men landed after such a storm and they were held captive by the one-eyed Cyclops (In Italian: Ciclope) before he outwitted him and blinded him.

The Cyclops, I recall, were a race of huge giants who lived in the caves of Etna and were pretty mean dudes. They ate people as appetizers.

Homer said after Ulysses blinded him, Poliphemus hurled two great boulders at the fleeing Greeks, as they were already sailing away, but he missed and the rocks landed in the waters off Acitrezza, fourteen kilometers away where they can be seen to this day as a reminder that Ulysses was the first foreigner to mistreat a native son of Sicily.

Yesterday was a re-creation of that day.

I was in Acicastello where I was using the internet at the Sheraton when a sudden wind came up. Then the rain. Then the wind and rain. Within fifteen minutes, gale force winds.

I wanted to see the sea and zipped my coat and walked a short distance to the water's edge.

The sky was an angry, dark, grey-black. By this time, the rain nearly horizontal. The wind-swept waves crashing onto the shore with unrelenting fury.

What a sight!

I immediately thought of Ulysses.

This must have been the kind of day that grounded him and his crew. I turned my back to the sea and looked behind me.

Etna loomed fourteen kilometers away, a straight shot.

"That guy Poliphemus must have been pretty pissed off at Ulysses if he threw two boulders fourteen kilometers at Ulysses," I thought to myself.

The rocks of Acitrezza are enormous. They jut out of the water maybe 60 feet high and are at least 30 feet in diameter.

They are cone-shaped and taper off to nearly a point at the top.

To hurl a couple boulders that size. Wow.

Then again, the Cyclops used to eat sheep whole, and also humans too, so we are talking a big fella here, plus he was the son of

Poseidon, the god of the ocean, so he has little god-blood in there somewhere.

Returning to the condo, I battened down all the hatches. For hours the wind wailed and the rains came down.

No way was I going out tonight.

Ulysses.

Gotta read that section in the *Odyssey* again.

I think it really happened. What a guy.

Chapter Six

Healing Days

1. A Healing day

This afternoon I took a drive to my ancestral village of Trecastagni, about half way up Mt. Etna.

The day was cloudy, and the mountain was hidden by dense clouds. Rain clouds.

As I proceeded up the mountain—a trip I have taken a thousand times—finally I felt at home. It took three days for the tension and fast pace of America to fade away.

On the side of the road, peddlers were selling grapes, persimmons, cactus pears (*fichidindia*), and artichokes. The same guys wearing the same clothes from the last time I was here, I swear. You know the picture: scruffy-faced men with those Italian caps, beat up worsted suits, a cigarette dangling out of their mouths.

I stopped the car and for three euros I picked up a kilo of grapes and four persimmons. Yummy. Tonight, I will eat them.

After a fifteen minute drive on the winding and narrow road, after passing new constructions here and there, I arrived in Trecastagni.

I was there for a reason that day. One of my dear friends from Massachusetts, a devotee of Sant Alfio, was having a hard time with a business investment. He was on the verge of losing everything. Last week, he stopped by the store and we talked. I told him that I would say a prayer for him and his family. Plus, I always stopped by at the Church of Sant'Alfio to say a prayer fro my two grandfathers, who were raised there, plus my dad. I have this prayer routine, as we all do. Basically, I start from the top and name just about everyone I know, and ask Sant'Alfio to intercede on their behalf.

Not that I am a religious fanatic, far from it. I have sinned so much in my life (I am a lawyer after all), that not only is he going to have to go to bat for me when I hit those pearly gates, but just about the entire congregation of saints will have to, as well.

I got to the Church as 3:00 PM and it was closed. I asked a worker (they are re-doing the facade and four workers were on staging, working like bees) at what time the church opened. He told me at 4:00 PM.

I had an hour to kill, so I headed to the town square for an espresso and to see the old timers there.

They gather at the square all day long and solve the world's problems, as countless Sicilians have done in countless village squares for millennia.

Taking my spot on a bench, I enjoyed the ambiance. The air was fresh, clean. Mountain air. On that bench, I thought of Alfio, my grandfather. He used to come at this very place as a teenager before emigrating to the USA. I thought of him, wondering if he ever sat on the bench that I was sitting on.

The palm trees were calm. The roses in the square a vibrant red, pink. The water monument in the square's center shut off for the winter ahead.

Fall in Trecastagni.

This moment was worth nine months of hard work back home.

At 4:00 o'clock I returned to the Church, and said my prayers.

I felt good in that place, a certain healing takes place, I think.

After a 30 minute visit, I left and headed to Viagrande to the pastry shop, and picked up a cannoli for a treat later that night.

Back on that mountain road I thought to myself: "This is why I come here".

2. Springtime Inspection

Spring has sprung and the mountains and fields of the Island are a panorama of colors, textures and scents as the earth comes alive after a very short winter's nap. Driving around the base of Mt. Etna in the springtime through the villages and towns and witnessing each town's preparation for the tourist season and coming summer months takes three or four hours by car since the circumference of Etna totals perhaps 50 miles.

My spring inspection tour begins by driving from my villa in Aci San Filippo (located next to Acireale) to Giarre. Giarre is a short trip on the *Autostrada* and is a wonderful town noted for its antique shops and yellow, textured terra cotta houses. The buildings are Baroque in inspiration and the imposing Duomo (cathedral) is a splendid example of the period's architecture.

Hugging the coast I head up the mountain to Linguaglossa, a dark, mysterious village literally built on top of a lava flow of centuries ago. The lava stone streets and houses are with their charcoal grey texture contrasts with the pantheon of colors of the hillside. Visiting the Bosco di Linguaglossa (Woods of Linguaglossa) is a wonderful excursion in itself, as trees and wildlife abound with pinks, reds, yellows, greens and violets exploding in the fresh growth vegetation.

Pulling into the ancient medieval town of Randazzo on the back side of the mountain, only a few minutes drive from the crater of Europe's highest volcano, Etna, it is time for a quick *panino* and something cold to drink. There is nothing quite like munching on a tomato, prosciutto and cheese *panino* drizzled with olive oil while gazing down from the mountain to the towns below. The freshly brewed espresso "lungo" completes the treat, and then I continue on.

Continuing on the backside of the mountain, magical Bronte is next. Noted for its pistachio trees and "fichidindia", scrumptious cactus pears introduced to Sicily by the Spanish, Bronte is a marvel of neatness and order. Surely it was the unique Bronte pistachio which was referred to in Genesis "...take in your bags some of our land's best products as a gift to this man: balsam, syrup, gum, laudanum, pistachio nuts and almonds" (Gen:43.11).

Circling down the mountain we run into Paternò, once part of the notorious "Triangulu di la morti" (Triangle of death). Decades ago this town, along with Belpasso and Misterbianco, comprised the area of Sicily featured in myths and legends, reminiscent of America's Wild West. Today, literally a bee hive of activity, Paternò has some of the best organic honey farms in Europe and tourists flock to the area for its treasure.

Continuing my inspection, I arrived at Misterbianco which was completely destroyed by a consuming lava flow in 1669 and drive past the town's ancient symbol, lava rock crowned with an iron cross, and reflect on the awesome power of Etna's wrath. Contrasting the old with the new, I stopped into the Italian version of Wal-Mart, "Auchon," and check how far the area has progressed into the 21st century.

Zipping home on the *Autostrada*, skirting Catania, a beautiful dark lava colored city the size of Boston and home to countless cultures and civilizations and twice destroyed by lava flows, I get caught in rush hour traffic. Soft, Italian pop music plays on the radio of my car. Gazing at the palm trees and greenery, waiting to push on, I think to myself, "Al, you've just driven 50 miles across a living museum...how great is that?"

Chapter Seven

Humor

1. The Suave and Debonair American

I am hobbling around like a one-legged woodpecker today.

Yesterday the heat was oppressive, so I decided to go to Viagrande to swim in the pool at the Hotel Madonna d'Oliva, where for a fee of 6 euros, you can swim in their new Olympic pool.

After paying the fee, I was told that I had to wear a bathing cap, which they conveniently sold for 3 euros. Thus, for 9 euros, about 13 bucks, I would get a little relief from the hot weather.

Had I thought about it for a little bit, I should have sat in my bath tub and saved 13 bucks, but at the time it seemed like a good idea.

Anyway, I found a nice "lettino" (lounge chair) with a nice umbrella, put on my new Speedo hat (I looked like a torpedo, really), and jumped in the azure blue pool.

What a relief.

I did a few laps nice and slow.

Until a pigeon dive bombed my hat.

Yup, right in the middle of a new Olympic pool in Viagrande, in front of a whole bunch of Sicilian mom and dads, I was pooped on by a thirsty and hot white pigeon.

What a revolting development.

Anyway, then I sheepishly stepped out of the pool trying to maintain a semblance of dignity, I slipped on a flip-flop that a kid had left at the top of the ladder.

Visualize this: a 240 pound guy who looks like a torpedo now doing a split like John Travolta did (no…better) on Saturday Night Fever.

Of course, I pulled my groin muscle.

Of course, it took me ten minutes to get up.

Of course, everyone thought that I was a comedian hired by the hotel, as everyone was now in hysterics.

Yup, your favorite sophisticated, debonair man of the world now with pigeon poop on the top of his torpedo head and hobbling back to his *lettino* with a pulled groin.

Anyway, I slithered out of there and got in the car.

Ever try to depress a clutch in a stick shift car with a pulled groin?

Mamma Mia!

I ended up driving home using one foot, an accomplishment that will now rank as one of my life's best feats, and hobbled into the house.

To make a humiliating story short, in the middle of the night because it was so hot I woke up and thought sand was in my throat. I went down the stairs to get some water when it happened: my left leg completely locked up on me.

So there I was, 4:00 o'clock in the morning, stuck in the middle of my staircase and I can't move a muscle.

Spying a mop by the the foot of the staircase, I reached for it and got it.

I decided to use it as a crutch and tried to get back upstairs.

As I climbed the first few steps, my girlfriend appeared at the top of the stairs.

"Alfred" she says "stop fooling around and come to bed!"

Twenty minutes later, I did.

Yup.

Another nice day in Sicily.

2. The Electric Gate

My new condo is located on a bluff overlooking Acitrezza, and has the most beautiful view in all of Sicily.

It is also a gated community, with an electric gate that allegedly keeps out the uninvited.

In reality, it keeps out the residents.

The first few times that I opened the gate with the key that you are supposed to insert into the key hole that allows the gate to open, there was no problem.

The last few days, though, the key hole there didn't work.

I had to jiggle the key about 100 times until it "caught," and then it finally opened.

"No way can you put up with this, Al! Especially if you have a couple drinks in you," I thought.

Calling Massimo, he suggested that we order two electric gate openers that you leave in the car. "It will take a few days" he said.

Last night I returned home late, and sure enough, the key didn't work.

After fifteen minutes of struggling with the damn thing, I decided to hop the fence and see if I could find some type of release lever.

Imagine an old fat guy like me trying to hop a five foot fence.

Well, I did it. After using the scientific method and deciding that all I had to do was park my car close to the gate, stand on the hood and jump on the fence, I decided to give it a try.

I maneuvered the car horizontally so it was parallel to the fence. That maneuvering took me fifteen minutes.

Finally, I got it right.

Perfect parking job.

Stepping out of the car, I took my shoes off (didn't want to scratch the paint job of the brand new Fiat 500 I was driving.....great car by the way). I kneeled on the hood and slithered up onto the roof.

Of course, my weight promptly dented the roof.

"You idiot," I thought.

From the roof, I straddled the fence. At this point I has half on one side and half on the other. Just as I was about to make the five foot drop, an old timer walked by.

"What are you doing up at this time of night?" he said.

I explained that the key didn't work and that I was hopping over the gate to open it from the inside.

"Why don't you just push the emergency button?" he said as he walked over to the fence and pushed it.

The gate began to open with me on top of it.

"Crap!" I said.

I jumped off and landed on a small rock. With no shoes, it hurt like hell.

The old guy just shook his head and said "Americano?"

I said, "Sì!"

He just shook his head and walked away.

Limping back to the car, I decided that tomorrow I'd better fix that roof.

3. My Little Putt-Putt

I am in love with my rent a car. As a matter of fact, someday I will buy one just like this one.

It is a Fiat.

Yes, yes, I know. Americans think Fiat stands for "Fix It Again, Tony," but really, they have come a long way, baby.

The model that I am driving is the Fiat 500. Last year it was Europe's "Car of the Year," and I think it would sell like hot cakes in America.

It is not a big car: two normal people can fit comfortably up front, and two hobbits likewise in the back, but for me, it is great.

First off, it is a diesel, which means that it sips fuel. Usually, diesel cars have no zip, but this one is a peppy little number. I can now go through the five speed shift like Mario Andretti.

The radio works, it has a CD, even power windows. Everything is great.

Except the color.

Bright (I mean bright) yellow. Banana yellow. Shiny banana yellow.

Why someone would paint a car bright, banana yellow is beyond me.

The benefit of a banana yellow car, however, is that it is very easy to find. The reason? Well, no one in all of Sicily has a banana yellow car except me.

More than once this week people have come up to me after I have parked this mini-chariot and have told me "Nice car" as they wipe the tears from their eyes.

What? Has no one ever seen a big guy with his head touching the roof inside shifting like a banshee driving a banana, yellow car?

I don't understand.

It also has somewhat of an effect on my social life too. No one will get inside the thing with me.

Even Maria Pace. I picked her up last night for pizza, and she ducked down in the front the whole time.

She said something about not wanting to be seen by her friends. Geez.

To me, a car is something that goes backward and forward. It gets me from point A to point B.

Now, I have to color coordinate?

Yup. I love my little Putt Putt. My banana yellow, shiny new one of a kind, state of the art auto.

Now I understand why Hertz is number one. All the others really have to try harder, I think.

4. Sicilian Men

Man, do I feel inferior around some Sicilian men. The very old guys, 80 or 90 years old, I can handle, but I never have seen a concentration of such good looking men in my life, I swear. Svelte, swagger, sex appeal. All with big chests. I wonder why?

Most of the business guys I know in Sicily my age (fifty something) and guys in their forties dress like they belong in GQ. Same thing.

My Eddie Bauer wardrobe is useless here. Plus, they look better than me.

Never do I see jeans, polos, sandals, flip–flops except at the beach.

Elegant casual wear is the rule of thumb for these guys.

Why? I needed to do research. I discovered the reason. Here's the reason: I have written in the past of going to the beach. Even fat guys wear those tiny pooch time speedo bathing suits.

Somehow, even the fat guys look good. Except me, of course.

Me? Forget it. I am a boxer guy and a boxer swim suit guy, no if, ands or buts about it. You will never catch me in pooch pants. Never. Not this guy. Nope.

I remember one time I lost my luggage. In those days I didn't leave behind a complete wardrobe like I do now.

After three days of no luggage, I figured I should buy some underwear as mine were by now walking to the chair, folding themselves, and generally waiting for the next use.

"Hmm..." I said. "Better do something fast!"

Off I went in the search for XXL boxers. (I could squeeze into XL in America, but I really like room to move if you know what I mean, and always buy bigger.)

I went to Scarringi in Misterbianco, a store like a Marshall's here in the states.

I searched high and low for boxers. Nothing but pooch pants.

In desperation, I asked for help. "Americano? " I was asked. "Sì" I said.

"Here" she said.

"God, they're tiny" I thought to myself. "Are you sure they are XXL? " I asked.

"Si."

So I bought four pair.

Taking them home and trying them on, they ripped at the knees as I was tugging. Couldn't even get them up half way. Yikes!

Fortunately, my bags arrived with fresh re-enforcements soon after, but when I brought those boxers home and gave them to my son Matt, who wears size medium, they were skin tight on him.

Now I know why Sicilian men are built like a Greek God. Their underwear pushes up everything, usually to the chest.

That's the reason they all have big chests. Tight underwear.

It pushes up everything. Brilliant!

Thus, I had a principled decision to make: "Do I wear tight underwear to be just like "them", or am I more of a swinging, free spirit type of guy, so to speak?"

Hey…I am American. We like things big. Forget the big chest. My wardrobe now has 14 pairs of clean, Eddie Bauer boxers, size XXL waiting for me. Made in America.

So while Sicilian men are fine, I still like the "Made in America" brand a tad better!

We are made of the "Real Stuff," I think.

5. Rocking With Bonnie

I will tell you a deep dark secret: music is my life. I love all types and what I listen to depends on that particular mood I am in that day.

Music influences my writing, which is vitally important to my sanity.

I came here two weeks ago in desperate need of spiritual recharging and music releases the creative writing side of me.

Thus, I came here with 791 of my favorite songs loaded in my I POD. A diverse collection of stuff ranging from Classical, Rock, Standards, Motown, Alternative, even a little rap, and of course, Bonnie.

All my friends accompanied me here…John Fogarty, Bob Marley, Amy Winehouse, the Wicked Picket, Sinatra, and of course the love of my musical life: Bonnie Raitt. I packed 59 of my favorite Bonnie tunes into my I POD, and this has been a Bonnie trip.

Bonnie and I go back almost four decades. I first heard her as a teenager at the Club 47 in Cambridge, and have been with her thru 33RPM records, eight tracks, cassettes, Cds…and now my IPOD.

From the first that I gazed on her and listened to her music and words, she moved my soul and my spirit.

It seems that it has always been Bonnie and me. Always. Through thick and thin.

Why, she even perspired on me once too.

Yup. My sister Anna has been in show business for a long time and always booked Bonnie at The Club Casino in Hampton, NH and later at the Oakdale Theater in Connecticut, where she booked all the talent.

Anna is very well known in the entertainment industry and someone that I admire for all her accomplishments. She is one of my heroes, actually.

Anyway, one time Bonnie was at the Casino, and my sister put me in a table directly under her microphone.

During the performance, she perspired in me. Three tiny drops fell on me: Rock and Roll Holy Water.

A couple years ago, Anna booked Bonnie at the Oakdale, and as a surprise for me, she arranged a back-stage meeting after the show.

I pecked Bonnie on the cheek and said to her "Bonnie…I have been listening to you since eight tracks. Thank you" She said to me "Wow! I am glad to see another old person here tonite". For a minute there, the years peeled back and I was at the Club 47 again.

I have a picture of that event somewhere in a drawer back home.

Anyway, here is the point: while I have been here, I have been rocking with Bonnie every single morning on my deck. Yup. She and I and my air guitar, and me shirtless and in my boxer shorts.

Not her soulful tunes. Those tug on my heart. Rather the rock stuff. The uplifting, kiss-ass rock and roll stuff.

You need to visualize two things in order to appreciate what happened to me this morning.

First, have you ever seen that bloody movie "Reservoir Dogs?".

It's a bloody Quentin Tarantino thing that is awful except for this one scene where one of the bad guys was torturing someone. He was doing a dance, kind of going back and forth to really cool music, while he was doing his thing.

He looked really cool in that scene, and it became a famous scene.

Well, that's the way I dance. That Lawrence, Boston, New York City–kind of urban dance thing.

I put on my IPOD, my earphones, my white fedora with black trim, and keyed up my favorite Bonnie rock song: a duet that she did with Bryan Adams called "Rock Steady," really one of the best pure rock tunes ever, shirtless and in my boxers and went on my deck.

Anyway, there I am this morning: a brilliant sunny Sicilian morning with an unlimited view of the sea and panorama below, warm and, well unbelievable, and here I am in my hat, I POD, and in boxers to boot, wailing to that tune.

Today, I was singing both parts of the song: I was rocking. I was the Reservoir Dogs guy, wailing my air guitar, dancing up a sweat, becoming one with that song, in another zone, another time, another galaxy. I was rocking and feeling really, really great.

Here's the opening of the song:

Bryan Adams: You need a man that'll treat you like the woman you are......those little boys are just fooling around with your heart....

Bonnie: What you gonna do now that you are all alone...You need a Rock, not a rolling stone...

Bryan: So when a boy just ain't enough...you need a man made of stronger stuff. So get ready...

Both: Rock steady all night long...rock steady 'til the break of dawn...Rock steady....

Man, was I flying. High with no drugs. In THE ZONE. Ever feel that way? The world was great this morning.

Me, my hat, my air guitar, Bonnie, and in my boxers, rocking like an eighteen year old.

Until my next door neighbor threw a pebble to get my attention, that is.

She's a nice lady, Mrs. Longo. She was sweeping her deck and noticed me. For about 10 minutes, she had put her broom down and was watching a crazy old American in boxer shorts rocking away with his ear phones and dancing like a mad man.

She threw a pebble at me to get my attention.

Shocked and embarrassed, I quickly took off the earphones and said: "Err...sorry, Mrs. Longo. I got carried away."

She said "No, no no, that was wonderful! Can I hear the song you were playing?"

I went inside my house and hooked up the IPOD to my speakers and brought them outside on the deck.

In no time there we were: me in my boxers, Mrs. Longo on her deck, me on mine, both dancing to Rock Steady with Bonnie.

It was totally awesome. She kept her clothes on, though. That's ok. She's a large woman and it would have wrecked the moment, I think.

Thus, me, Bonnie and old Mrs. Longo, rocking away on my deck in Sicily.

Who woulda thunk it?

6. The Key Tattoo…The Key!

Little things in life make me happy. A jug of wine, a loaf of bread and a shiny, new key to my electric gate in front of the condo.

Yessiree!

No more climbing the fence, no more tying the damn thing down, no more ringing buzzers to people that I do not know asking them to let me in.

Now, I have a shiny, new key that really works. The gate opens like magic. The family jewels are no longer at risk.

To add icing to the cake, by today I will have a shiny new "telecommando," a remote control that will automatically open the gate.

Yup, life couldn't be better.

Plus, yesterday I was a hero, too.

A combination of Arnold, Brad, Tom and Mel all rolled into one. Here's the story:

About 3:00 PM yesterday, as I was doing some very serious lounging on my deck, my Italian cell phone rang.

It was little Maria Pace.

"Alfred, help me," she said. "Someone tried to steal the motor scooter that I was using while I was in a restaurant, and broke the ignition. I can't tell my father as he will kill me. Can you please come and pick me up?" she asked.

Racing to my closet, I quickly donned my Superhero outfit.

Kinda like a cross between a Spiderman costume and a Superman, except in size XXL and having that super elastic waistband to keep the tummy in and push it to where the chest should be.

"I am coming, my dear" I said. "Where are you?"

After getting the directions to the place, I raced outside and jumped into the famous "Al Mobile"—my special souped up little Fiat 500 that is always in a state of readiness for just such an occurrence.

Driving to the electric gate (had not yet received my shiny, new key), I tried to leap over it with a single bound.

Once that didn't work, I climbed over it, but since the superhero costume was made of authentic Superhero fibers secretly made by Orazio Melanzana in a secret lab up on Etna, nothing ripped when I fell to the ground..

Quickly dusting off, I jumped back into the sleek Al Mobile and off I went.

Speeding thru hill and dale, I popped in my favorite CD from the battle scene of *Apocalypse Now* when the choppers attacked the village and thought to myself:

"Geez, I love the smell of orange trees in the morning!"

After a twenty minute drive, I found that beautiful damsel in distress.

She was sitting on the curb eating an ice cream.

Leaping out of the Al Mobile, I sang out "Here I come to save the day: Mighty Al is on the way!"

As I was about to start the second verse, Maria said to me "Alfred, you really are an idiot. You are embarrassing me plus your suit is ripped. Your butt is hanging out!"

"Ah...." I said, "And all this time I thought the fabric was tropical, so cool and airy!"

Driving back to the condo, content in performing another successful mission, I thought to myself "What a guy. If I could put me in a bottle, I'd be rich!"

Then I hummed the tune to Star Wars as I climbed the gate one last time.

Hanging the costume in my closet, I returned to my serious lounging again and waited for the cell to ring.

"Eternal Vigilance" I thought.

All I gotta do is keep saying that to myself, I think.

7. Frutta and Polyester

White mulberries.

Have you ever eaten them? The kind that are so juicy that they kinda squirt in your mouth as you chew them, sending you into a veritable ecstasy?

How about peaches that you have to eat with a napkin as they are just chock full of juice?

Better still, cantaloupe or Crawford melon, sweeter than I don't know what.

Better still: those tiny, wild mountain strawberries that you can smell six inches away from your mouth and then melt in your mouth.

Yup. The spring harvest is in, and boy, oh boy, am I eating healthy.

As a matter of fact, all of the above are in my fridge right now.

Close by my house is a green grocer. And it is now my favorite green grocer.

Actually, it's a she. Gabrielle.

She's so pretty that I'd buy fruit from here even if I hated the stuff. And her mom is even prettier. A mom and daughter operation.

Anyway, last January I befriended both of them. So I dropped by today to pick up some stuff. After greeting me with kisses on both cheeks (God, do I love that custom), she got down to business.

Here in Sicily, the grocer picks the fruit for you. You point to the ones you want. If you don't point to exactly what you want and leave it to the grocer, invariably one or two blemished ones or slightly over ripe once are thrown in the bottom of the bag, so you have to be like a hawk.

Anyway, Gabrielle picked out some real beauties for me. I was too busy looking at her, if you know what I mean, and she could have put in the kitchen sink for all I know, but since she is my friend, she usually gives me the best product.

Today the white mulberries had just come in from a nearby farm. They were plump and an inch long. I popped a few in my mouth and wow! What taste!

I hate buying fruit at Stop&Shop in America. Mealy peaches, tasteless berries, green melons that take forever to ripen, rock hard pineapple is what I usually end up with, so this stuff is really a treat for me.

I then stopped by the *panificio* (bread shop) to pick up a few loaves of bread for the next couple days too. I bought one brioche to have with coffee tomorrow morning: brioche, coffee, fruit: my breakfast for the next couple of days. The breakfast of champions.

I stopped by the Sheraton Hotel in Acicastello to use their internet café, too. I actually bumped into some Americans from Miami who were here for three days before heading to Rome. Three old ladies who belonged in a bingo hall in some church parish, to be honest and had the bluest of blue hair.

One of them complained "I can't find a decent piece of meat here and no one speaks English". When I suggested to her that nowadays no one speaks English in Miami, she glared at me and waddled away.

I think that Italy has outlawed that much polyester on a person at one time, but I didn't mention that at least.

I returned home to rest up because later on I went to a Sicilian disco in order to do "social research" for my next blog piece.

The place is supposed to be killer, but it opens at 1:00 am.

The last time I was up that late was New Year's Eve, but I lasted only until 12:15 then.

Wonder if I can stay up that late. I'll give it the old try, though.

All work in the name of social research, of course.

8. The Sicilian Hot Dog

I love hot dogs. Despite the fact that they are made from every conceivable body part of every conceivable animal, I am a hot dog aficionado.

However dumb that sounds, it is true. Give me a couple dogs on the grill with a little mustard and relish, ad I am a happy camper. Yesterday I had an overwhelming desire for the Mighty Dog, so I decided to hunt a couple down.

Walking into this new supermarket that I found near the condo called A&O, I began my quest for the Perfect Dog.

I headed to the condiment aisle first. Locating the mustard, I thought to myself that this would be a snap.

However, no relish. Heck, I didn't even know how to say "relish" in Italian, and I kept getting directed to the pickle department. Ketchup, yes. Mayo, yes. But what good gourmand puts either on the Mighty Dog?

Only heretics, I thought.

Resigning myself to the fact that tonight my supper would be sans relish, I headed to the bread aisle in search of hot dog rolls.

Right. Nice try.

Nothing resembling a hot dog roll existed. Not even a hamburg roll for that matter. Settling on something that was at least soft, kinda thick, kinda long, I threw it into my basket and headed to the deli.

There, I found fifty kinds of cheeses. Ten kinds of salamis. Countless hams, prosciutttos, mortadella: a veritable delight of cold meats to be sure, but no hot dogs.

I asked the attendant: "Dove sono gli hot dog?" He smiled and said "Americano?"

I said, "Sì".

Pointing to the cold case department, he smirked and walked away.

I knew what he was thinking: What kind of a dolt would eat a hot dog in Sicily?

I knew that but by quest to find the Mighty Dog would continue, no matter what anyone thought.

There, nestled in the extreme right hand corner of the cold case, I found them. Three different kinds: Beef, pork, and who knows what else. Of course, I picked the least healthful one. The pork dogs. They were big, they looked juicy. My mouth watered.

Rushing back to the condo, I searched high and low for the grill.

Missing. Probably discarded by the movers. I hadn't used it much in six years anyway.

My choices were either frying in oil or boiling the noble ones.

I chose the American way: boiling.

Opening the pack, I selected two of the best looking candidates, washed them and threw them into the pot.

Then the unbelievable occurred. They grew in size!

Really. They grew. And grew. These babies were gigantic. By the time they were cooked, these wonders were nearly eight inches long and two inches round. I couldn't believe it.

They looked like two brown rubber hoses.

Plus, the whole house smelled.

"Houston, we have a problem" I thought.

Sticking a fork into one of those humongous babies, I placed it into the "roll". Giving it a good dose of mustard (really, this stuff, when I squirted it was a pale yellow, almost white).

With great trepidation, I took a bite.

Oh, my God.

I swallowed a biteful of I don't know what.

Watery sponge. Meat flavored mush. Gooey crapola.

The Mighty Sicilian Dog had turned out to be an imposter. A cheap imposter that resemble a hot dog, but that's it.

The guy who made this dog should be arrested for impersonating a manufacturer, I thought. Then shot.

Later that evening, as I sat in Salvo's restaurant eating a nice dish of *Pasta a la Norma* (pasta with eggplant), I thought to myself: "Alfred, sell American dogs in Sicily...you'd clean up. The Sicilians eat McDonalds, now Burger King too. Why not hot dogs?"

I then got a visual of myself standing in the central Duomo in Catania, surrounded by hordes of tourists with one of those stainless steel hot dog carts yelling "Hot dogs, get your American hot dogs!"

Putting down my forkful of delicious pasta, I then thought to myself "Alfred, that idea is almost as dumb as the last idea you had," which, of course, I will not disclose to yet as litigation is not yet underway.

Anyway, my quest for the perfect dog now only a fond memory, I decided to stick to the local fare, unless I can find the perfect hamburg, that is!

Chapter Eight

Musings

1. Standing Our Ground Now and Forever

Recently, the airwaves have been filled with all sorts of talk about Italians, some of it not so good.

Snippets of a sermon recently surfaced when a pastor of an inner city church said: "[Jesus'] enemies had their opinion about Him. The Italians for the most part looked down their garlic noses at the Galileans" The same gentleman called Jesus' crucifixion "a public lynching Italian style" executed in "Apartheid Rome".

Of course, you'd have to be living under a rock someplace not to have heard that comment on the television, as it has been played and re-played thousands of time now.

Not that I give one whit about what this gentleman thinks about my Sicilian/Italian background, nor do I particularly believe anything that comes from the mouths of most politicians (they are, after all, politicians), who have attempted to exploit that comment one way or the other for their own purposes, but I began to wonder about persecution and discrimination against Italians in America, and I was saddened to find scores of examples of discrimination and persecution against Italian and Sicilian people. I am not talking about the recent "mafia" stuff done to our detriment by the "Soprano's", The Godfather Trilogy", or "Goodfella's " either.

As far back as the 16th century, John Calvin, the French reformer who helped establish the Reformed Church of Switzerland, condemned Italians as lazy, two-faced, and deceitful.

Here in America, did you know that the largest lynching in American history involved Sicilians?

After the American Civil War, poor Italian immigrants were recruited in the South by plantation owners desperate for laborers and in the North by rich industrialist looking to fill their sweat shops with cheap labor.

In the South, fisherman from Sciacca and the fishing villages of Sicily settled in Louisiana because of the climate and in the hopes of securing work on both the plantations and also to fish for shrimp, plentiful in the Gulf of Mexico waters.

48

Over time, however, resentment grew against these new settlers. Some Americans viewed these poor immigrants as some sort of a "missing link" between fair skinned Europeans and Africans.

In no time, violence against Italian immigrants boiled over and discrimination became rampant.

In 1891, ten Sicilians were lynched in New Orleans, Louisiana. Yes, that is correct: lynched.

The largest lynching in American history perpetrated against Sicilians!

In researching the incident, I found out that the chief of police in New Orleans, a fellow named Hennessey, was assassinated under dubious circumstances. Some say he was investigating the Mafia. Most others now believe that he was involved in some other political intrigue and was executed by others who blamed the Sicilians.

It was alleged that on his death bed he said "The Dagos did it".

Nineteen Sicilians were rounded up, and jailed. Ten were accused of Hennessey's murder.

Rumors swirled through the city that the Mafia was trying to take over New Orleans. The local newspapers chipped in by fanning hatred toward the new immigrants with terrible and hateful articles.

The ten accused of murder were acquitted at trial, but that didn't stop mobs of people incited by those hateful newspaper articles.

A large riot broke out. Rioters stormed the jailhouse where they were being held and according to newspaper accounts 'The lynch mob brutally mutilated the Italian immigrants, shouting, "Hang the dagos!" According to the newspaper, the "cheers were deafening."

The paper proclaimed "The little jail was crowded with Sicilians, whose low, receding foreheads, repulsive countenances and slovenly attire proclaimed their brutal nature."

I was angered when I first read these accounts, then saddened. I was angered as a proud Sicilian, yet saddened by the ignorance of the uneducated, led just like sheep to the wrong conclusion by the court of public opinion.

But that wasn't the end of my research. Four years later, in 1895, six Italian labor organizers were lynched in Colorado, and another six were lynched in Hahnville, Louisiana. Another five more were lynched in 1899 in Tallulah, Florida. The list went on.

In 1901, mobs attacked and killed Italians in Mississippi. In 1906 the same occurred in West Virginia. In 1910 the same occurred in Tampa, Florida.

In Westford, Illinois, an incident occurred against Italians there that was so horrible that historian John Higham wrote "No pogrom has ever stained American soil, nor did any single anti-Jewish incident in the 1920's match the violence of the [vigilante mob-led] anti-Italian riot".

I realized that less than 100 years ago, Italians were killed for being Italians. I was shocked.

The hate and resentment toward Italians was also fueled, in addition to ignorance and bigotry, by religion, of all things.

Italians were Catholics, Papists, whose real loyalty was to the Pope, and not to America.

Protestant societies fueled resentment everywhere. Catholics were considered perverse, immoral, drank excessive alcohol, and they gambled. They weren't "like us."

Thus, a picture of resentment and hatred was painted against the new immigrants. A perverse picture fueled by the ignorant and the rich, hell-bent on preserving their way of life, and aided and abetted by "religious" bigotry, as well.

As is the case with hostile racial or ethnic stereotypes, contributions of Italians to America and the world in countless areas, (arts, music, science, mathematics, government , and law) were forgotten or deliberately ignored.

The discrimination against Italians has not ended. Bu we as Italians and Sicilians need to be alert and not allow a repetition of the past abuses. We must stand our ground now and in the future to preserve who we are.

But we too should never forget.

2. Re-Inventing Ourselves

With reference to movies such as the *The Godfather, Goodfellas, The Bronx Tale,* and to television programs such as the *Sopranos,* I am one of those Sicilian-Americans who believes that over the past couple of decades, this particular genre of films has set back the U.S.'s view of Italians in general and Sicilian-Americans in particular.

While perhaps appreciating them as "artistic" films, other than to spark an interest in the "badda-bing" type of commercial exploitation, they have done nothing to enhance the awareness throughout the U.S. of the greatness that Italians in general and Sicilians in particular have brought to this world. Sadly, many prominent Italian-American directors, producers and actors have lined their pockets and are now fabulously wealthy as a result of this exploitation, and Oscars line the mantles in their homes.

Last year I received a call from a prominent advertising agency in New York City. The woman at this agency asked me if *All Things Sicilian* would be interested in taking part in a giant press conference announcing the release of a new DVD game. They were interested in giving out gift baskets filled with our products to "famous" people who were going to participate in the grand marketing event, which included the press, and therefore would be an excellent exposure for our products.

During the conversation, she told me that they were also soliciting a fedora manufacturer (a hat maker), a cigar manufacturer, and a mattress manufacturer. Puzzled, I asked her for the name of this new DVD game. She proudly told me...*The Godfather*...home DVD edition.

Feeling affronted, I lectured her on our rich culture and expressed my offense by her marketing agency and the manufacturer.

I hung up the phone, upset at this senseless exploitation.

At the time, I issued a press release condemning the release of the game and contacted various Italian-American organizations who likewise did the same. My press release was never published, and only scant attention was given to those published by the other Italian-American organizations.

Fast forward now one year.

Last week while reading the newspaper one night, I read a story about the sales of this particular game. It is now one of the best selling DVD games available for home use. According to the article, you can work your way up the criminal organization to the status of a "Don" by killing this person or that person, stealing this or that, or robbing this person or that person. Reading this article truly saddened me.

This genre has entered the fabric of our society permanently. The extensive contributions that creative, hard working Italian-Americans, doctors, lawyers, businessmen, artists, professors, poets, the list goes on forever, are negated by this shameless exploitation of our cultural background.

Heroes like Professors Gaetano Cipolla from Arba Sicula and Joseph Privitera who have dedicated their lives educating Americans on who a Sicilian really is, are beacons in this area of darkness.

We all need to be beacons. We need to learn about our background, really learn about it and understand from where we came and what we can truly accomplish in order to reverse this inaccurate perception.

Who are we? We are Sicel, we are Phoenician, we are Greek, we are Roman, we are Arab, we are Norman, we are Byzantine, we are English, we are Spanish, blended into one culture: an example for all the world to see, that's who we truly are. We have to learn about our history first, and then teach our children and our grandchildren. We must never forget who we truly are.

3. Tough Times

Like many Americans, I have been glued to the TV following our nation's financial crisis. Politicians have been scaring everyone with visions of another Great Depression. Everyone is fearful of losing jobs, homes and personal retirement funds. When our grandfathers and grandmothers came to this country, many had nothing with them except a small bag of personal possessions, the clothes on their back, and a vision of a new start in life. They lived in cramped apartments, often with no heat. They had no cars. They had no insurance, retirement or pension. There were no offices for unemployment, welfare or social security. Heck, almost all of them spoke no English. They worked seven days a week in sweatshops. Their kids came home every day to empty apartments in run-down sections of town while their parents slaved away.

Our grandparents were constantly victimized, discriminated against by "True Americans"; they had tough, tough lives. They sacrificed themselves for the American Dream. Not all realized this dream, but many did. Today, as a descendant of these pioneers who threw themselves into a foreign way of existence, I have to ask myself: "Do we have what it takes to overcome adversity like they did? Do we remember what they did for us? Can't we do it too? Isn't that heroic DNA also flowing in our veins?"

Today, more than ever, we need that spirit of our ancestors as we face these tough economic times. We need to reflect upon our roots and where we are today. What we have now, even in these "tough" times, is light years ahead of what they had. Many of us are educated. Many of our children and grandchildren are educated. American business, education, arts, sciences, mathematics, every industry is full of Italian and Sicilian Americans who have achieved success. This success was earned despite starting from nothing. Now I ask you:—especially during Italian and Sicilian Cultural Heritage Month—"has this spirit died? Has the sacrifice of millions of our ancestors been for naught?"

No way. This country will recover. It will recover in part because of a spirit instilled in us by example, the spirit of hard work, sacrifice and that "never give up" attitude that our forefathers brought with them through Ellis Island. We have something that many are desirous of: our inbred spirit. We are survivors.

As I think of our grandfathers and grandmothers —all heroes to me— and the profound sacrifices that they made on my behalf, I can say proudly that I am an American, and I will not let them down, now or ever. Together, as Americans, proud Americans, we must do whatever we have to do to ensure that the success earned through their sacrifices made long ago will continue for generations to come.

4. Journey of Discovery

People have often asked me "Al, why the fixation with Sicily?" Here is my response. Until 1996, I had never been to Sicily. I had been to Rome, London, and Paris, but never to Sicily. I was busy with my law practice, teaching at three Boston law schools, and bringing up my three children.

A vacation for me in those days was a week in Newport, Rhode Island or a trip on the road to follow my beloved Boston College football team, or a vacation in Chicago to listen to America's best jazz and blues. My life was orderly, but also dreary and dull. Despite the fact that I was considered successful professionally something inside of me was incomplete.

In late 1996, my father, Santo, took ill. He was the original "latch-key" kid. His parents (my grandparents) had emigrated from Sicily early in the 20th century and worked in the sweat shops of Lawrence, Massachusetts, seeking a better life, just like hundreds of thousands of other Sicilians. He often came home to an empty house after school and only Sicilian was spoken in the house. He was a Depression Era kid. Thus, he was a bilingual, latch-key kid, although in those days that term wasn't used.

As he lay dying in the hospital, I spent a lot of time with him. We had always been close and we talked about successes and failures in his life and mine. They were philosophical musings of a man trying to make peace with himself before passing. He told me that he never had the opportunity to visit Sicily, that he had been too busy trying to "stay afloat" in life, and that he regretted not saying a prayer for his father Alfio in the Church of Sant'Alfio in Trescastagni. He died a peaceful death in December of 1996 never having fulfilled that wish.

As a good son, I promised myself that I would fulfill my dad's dream. Two months later, I stepped off a plane for the first time in Sicily. I clearly remember looking out the window as the plane circled Fontanarossa Airport in Catania. The plane circled over Mt. Etna, and I was awestruck by its enormity and beauty.

When we landed and deplaned, as soon as my feet touched the tarmac at the airport, every DNA molecule in my body screamed "Alfred, you are home." I had a wondrous, spiritual experience that first trip. I paid homage to my father (and grandfathers) by praying for their souls at the Church of Sant'Alfio. I hunted down my grandparents' ancestral homes. I found the graves of long-lost relatives. I smelled the sweet Sicilian air, hungry to make up for lost years and time.

I returned home a completely different man. I decided to change my life. I found Massimo and created a law partnership in Catania with him and I bought a villa in Pachino. That first year, I returned to Sicily three times. Since then, I have spent more time there than here.

Two years later, perhaps one of the most significant events of my life happened. I brought my 80 year old mother and eldest daughter, Jennifer, to Sicily for Mom's birthday. I had a big surprise for her too: a memory that is burned in our minds. I had made arrangements with the current owner of my mom's ancestral home, the home of her mom and he gave us a tour of the house. I will never forget the look on Mom's face as she entered her mother's bedroom: th house was exactly as her mom had described to her, including the beautiful camellia tree in the front yard.

Over the years, I have brought all my kids there many times. My children know that I plan to retire in Sicily and be buried there.

In 1997, I rediscovered my roots: generations of my ancestors called me home and I thank the Lord every day that for once, I listened to somebody!

Chapter Nine

Massimo

1. Introduction

Massimo Grimaldi is my best friend and brother.

I met him almost ten years ago when I needed a Sicilian lawyer for a business matter and a fast and firm friendship soon developed.

When I decided to import Sicilian goods into America, he jumped at the chance to get involved, and we represented many Sicilian businesses over the years, helping them through the morass of American import law.

Over the years, our families merged and the business relationship mutated into a family relationship.

My children regard him as the older brother and he has visited America many times over the holidays when I am not in Sicily.

On all my activities in Sicily, he is my confidant, friend, adviser, translator and counselor.

His family in Sicily is now my family and I can say that truly he is a remarkable man.

The following essays are a snippet of some of the more humorous events that he and I have shared.

I actually have hundreds.

2. *Cosi di pazzi*

My Sicilian law partner, friend and brother, Massimo, has taken hosting a child's second birthday party to a new level.

Two weeks ago, his son Marzio celebrated his second birthday. Honestly, this kid looks like an angel. Next to my grandkids, I have not seen a more physically beautiful little boy. But to say he is a tad rambunctious is an understatement. I call him a "Dennis The Menace" clone. He is in front of you one second, out the door the next. Six eyes and five legs are needed to keep up with this "angel". When he gets that glint in his eyes, watch out!

Marzio is 100% Sicilian; yet, with his blond hair and blue eyes you'd think he was Irish or Dutch. He gets his looks from his parents. Massimo is the equivalent of a Sicilian Brad Pitt, and Anna (his wife) is so beautiful that sometimes I feel like I should pay for the view. Anyway, Massimo and Anna recently had a second child, a beautiful baby girl named Carola. Juggling jobs (Massimo is a lawyer, Anna, an economist), two little kids, along with a million other daily responsibilities, they haven't been able to share quality time together, not even to go out for a pizza. So Massimo gets the bright idea to hold a "festa" for Marzio.

All told 100 were invited to the festa: 60 little kids and 40 adults. "Alfred" he said "I will have a nice enjoyable time at my son's birthday."

Ya, right.

He hired a couple of Sicilian women to do the cooking, and inflated all the toys that he had carted back home from the US last November. (They were enormous inflatable bouncing things!). About one hour before the guests were to arrive, little Carola fell ill and Anna decided that she would have to stay in the bedroom to care for her, leaving Massimo to host the party alone. Just Massimo and 60 screaming little kids along with his own Dennis the Menace.

Let me add here that Massimo is a neat freak. Yup. Every time there is a tiny smudge on a window, he gets out the Windex and cleans it. He arranges his closet by color; his house looks is a museum, expensive art work, antique furniture, fragile decorative figurines everywhere. You get the picture?

The screaming hordes arrived. The invasion of the Sicilian banshees. Kids ran everywhere yelling, screaming, dropping ice cream, cake, candy wherever they stepped. Massimo spent the day opening the front door, chasing his son, picking up the spilled stuff, and generally experiencing a complete parental meltdown.

Dennis the Menace, meanwhile, was doing his thing too which was generally to cause havoc. After four hours, the hordes departed as quickly as they had descended.

"Massimo," I inquired the next day, "How was the party?"

"Alfred" he gasped." It was a very, very bad idea," he said. "I am completely exhausted! There is cassata cake everywhere and melted ice cream all over the place."

"Did Marzio have a good time?" I asked.

"I am still looking for him," he said.

I suggested that maybe next year he should take them to the Sicilian equivalent of Chuckie Cheese or Mc Donald's for a Happy Meal in order to make it a tad easier.

"Are you crazy, Alfred? he said. "Anna is already planning Carola's first birthday party. Anna told me that birthdays for little girls are even more important, and she wants to invite 150 people this time. Do you think I can come to America, please?"

Ah yes, the joys of Sicilian parenthood, exactly like here in America, no?

3. Lost in Translation!

Today it is snowing in New England.

It never snows in Sicily except on Mt. Etna, and that is for a short period of time only in January or February.

I remember the first time my friend and business partner Massimo came to America. It was late March and the weather forecast was for a light dusting that day, maybe an inch or so.

The morning he was leaving from Sicily, he called me and asked what the weather was. I told him that we were going to have a little snow when he arrived, no more than an inch, and he was happy to hear that as he had never experienced a "snowstorm". In Catania where he lives, it never snows. There are banana trees there, for heaven's sake.

In Sicily, it is a big deal if the weather dips into the 40's. People bundle up like it is sub-zero:. thick coats, hats, mittens: the whole gambit.

Anyway, when he came out of customs you have to picture this: he has on a fur Eskimo hat, tied around his chin. He had on a snow jacket worthy of a Mt. Everest climber. Fur mittens. Huge snow boots. He looked like that kid from that movie Christmas story after his mom dressed him up to go outside in winter. Hilarious.

I roared with laughter and so did the others waiting there for loved ones. Here I was with a light jacket on and Massimo dressed for the Blizzard of '78.

"Massimo" I said "I told you that we were expecting an inch of snow, not a foot" He looked at me funny. Then I realized that he had misunderstood me and thought that we were getting a meter of snow (over 3 feet) instead of an inch of snow.

Needless to say, for the rest of the trip we roared over that one.

Another time I called Massimo when we were having a blizzard, and Anna, his beautiful wife answered the phone. Massimo wasn't home. I told Anna that we were having a big storm and to have Massimo call me when he got home.

A couple hours later, Massimo called me and asked what I said to Anna. I told him that I told her that we were having a storm.

Now it was Massimo's turn to roar with laughter. "Alfred" Massimo said "Anna thought you said 'a stormo,' which means a large flock of birds. Anna wanted to know why there was a large flock of birds in America"

To this day, we both chuckle as we recall both stories!

4. The Banshee Kids

Dennis, the Sicilian Menace.

This kid can wear any five adults out. He's blond, angelic, probably the most beautiful Sicilian kid I have ever seen. However, don't let those beautiful looks of this precocious five year old fool you. Meet Marzio. The Sicilian Dennis the Menace.

He is the son of my law partner Massimo. Poor Massimo is exhausted, ready to pull his hair and going out of his mind with this hellfire. He has an associate, too. Mighty Might. Carola, his two year old sister.

Meet Anna, exhausted Anna. The beautiful wife of Massimo and mother of these two dynamos. Formerly the Sicilian version of Brad and Angelina, Massimo and Anna are now punch-drunk and wild-eyed.

So is the forty year old nanny that takes care of the kids. Fourth nanny.

Having a way with kids, I thought Massimo was exaggerating when he described the kids to me. "Don't worry, Massimo" I said. "I will play with them. I will settle the kids down so you and Anna can rest a little."

Ha.

Before I went to their place, a stately villa in Aci San Filippo if ever there was one, I stopped by the bookstore and purchased a coloring book, and a writing book. I got the coloring book for the girl and the writing book for the boy. I remembered this writing book myself as a child. It had each letter of the alphabet on a separate page along with a picture of something that began with that letter. "A" was AERO...airplane. Below the picture was the letter A along with space for the little tyke to practice printing that letter.

As a child, that book kept me occupied for hours. That little angel Marzio looked at the book for all of five seconds before throwing it on the floor and running for his plastic dinosaurs and transformers. Of course, one by one he threw them at me. Carola, when she saw that Disney coloring book of Sleeping Beauty, held up her fist and said to me in Italian "I will punch you" Hmm. For two hours these kids surrounded me and jumped, punched, pulled, spilled, harassed and attacked me. Finally, I dug deep into my memory and remembered what my famous uncle Harry used to do to me and my brother when we acted up. I tickled them. Yup.

I tickled their feet, their stomachs, I was a relentless tickler. From being on offense, they were now on defense. Zio Alfred was getting the upper hand. In any case, I'd say it was a draw with those kids. As I left the house, filled with every conceivable toy produced from China and America, I said a prayer of thanks. When I got home, Massimo called me.

"Alfred" he said. "My children really, really love you. They are crying for you. Can you believe this? This has never happened. I want to invite you over the house for Sunday dinner so you can play with them again." Geez. I accepted the invitation because Anna is a killer cook, but this time I am wearing my work out clothes. I do not think that the cleaner is going to be able to get out the wine stain and chocolate *gelato* stain on my new silk shirt that I wore tonight.

5. A Sicilian Shopping Spree!

In the past I have written about Massimo, my Sicilian law partner. Last week Massimo flew here from Sicily in order to assist us in developing new products for next spring (to launch a new product takes a lot of work, and Massimo's assistance is invaluable). While in the States, Massimo asked me if I could take him shopping on "Black Friday", and of course, I agreed.

I had thought it was odd when Massimo had hoisted three oversized suitcases into my van when I picked him up at the airport. Little did I know at the time what he had in mind.

No sooner had Massimo unpacked his bags on Wednesday night (before Thanksgiving), when he asked that I take him to Baby Gap and Old Navy to buy a "few" things for his two year old son, Marzio. At Baby Gap he wiped out the entire toddler section of boy's clothes —in addition to the great sale prices, his Euro were worth 50% more than our dollar. As I loaded his bags into my van, I regretted not having bought Gap Stock that morning.

Next stop: Old Navy —a repeat performance— an entire section of baby toddler clothes wiped out. Massimo explained to me that fleece clothing is not available in Sicily, and fleece kept his son warm on those cold January and February Sicilian days. Anything made of fleece went right into the shopping cart.

Next stop: Hallmark. Massimo's wife Anna loves the figurines called "Snow Babies". In years past we sent several to Anna and Massimo as Christmas gifts. Now, he has the biggest collection of Snow Babies in all of Europe! The manager of Hallmark wept with joy as she wrapped everything!

Next stop: Wal-Mart. Wal-Mart? The store was packed. No way was I going in. "I'll wait outside," I told him.

Twenty minutes later he came out with two huge carts full of enormous inflatable dolls and figures: Santa Clauses, Frosty the Snowmen, a Christmas village. Note I use the plural. Note also that these inflatable dolls were not "ordinary" inflatable dolls: one was over 15 feet long when inflated! Another was five feet in diameter! He was going to create a Winter Wonderland in Sicily for his son in the front yard!

As my truck bulged with gifts I wondered how the heck he was going to get everything home. He spent four hours packing everything in canvass bags, each four feet long by three feet wide.

On Sunday, I dropped him off at the airport. He had so much stuff that the airplane practically could not get off the ground! He arrived in Sicily on Monday and by Tuesday his Christmas Village was on display, brought to Sicily via America ! Santa does in fact fly all over the world, I thought.

The newspapers have reported that retail sales were up more than expected the first few days of the Christmas selling season due to the fact that Europeans and Canadians are flocking here to buy goods because of the weak dollar. Excellent news for the U.S. economy!

Massimo's story was repeated by thousands of other Europeans all over the States, and hopefully will be repeated even more in the coming weeks. The result? A thriving economy, a Sicilian child who will wear fleece clothes this winter and an entire neighborhood of Sicilian kids who will be amazed, awed, and excited by Massimo's wondrous Christmas display from America!

I am leaving for Sicily on December 24th. As I spend the holidays with Massimo and his family, I will think fondly of our "shopping spree' and see for myself the look of joy on his son's face as he experiences an American Christmas in Sicily!

Merry Christmas and Happy New Year!?

6. Sicilian Baptism

Last August I attended the baptism of Massimo's son Marzio, my first Sicilian "Feast". Here is a description of that wonderful day:

They weren't kidding when they say that Sicily is hot hot hot in August! The first two weeks of August are the hottest in Sicily and it takes a couple of days to get used to the heat.

After spending three weeks in the States, I returned to Sicily to attend the baptism of Massimo's son, Marzio. It was a mid-August sweltering hot day making me realize that sometimes the creature comforts here at home are hard to beat, such as air conditioning.

Before leaving for Sicily, I checked with Massimo regarding bringing a sports jacket for the event. "Alfred," he said, "Bring a suit as many people will be at the reception afterward and everyone will be very dressed up."

With this in mind, I packed my best suit, shirt and tie and zipped to Sicily. Well, actually, not exactly zipped to Sicily, kind of zagged there. As usual, Alitalia (short for Always Late in Take Off and Landing) went on strike exactly at the moment of check in at Logan, so I got switched to Lufthansa, which eventually got me to Sicily, but not before an eight hour stopover in Munich, Germany where I actually drank a glass of beer at 8 a.m. just to experience an authentic German beer.

Upon arrival in Sicily, the heat hit me like a club. 44 degrees Celsius. That's 102 degrees Fahrenheit. Marzio's baptism was the following day. My body had not yet adjusted to the heat and it was fighting jet lag. As I buttoned my shirt and threw on my tie, the sweat poured off me.

"Forget the dark blue shirt," I said to myself "wear the white one". Five shirts later, I jumped into the car and headed to Via Grande for the ceremony. Even though I love Sicilian churches, they are quaint, well preserved, down right holy. The one thing missing in just about all of them is an adequate air supply. The "air conditioning" consisted of a single little fan that was perched on a side altar, at the feet of Saint Anthony, 100 feet away! Looking around at the friends and family, I realized that I was the only one feeling so hot. Sicilians are used to heat and their bodies have adapted.

Every woman looked beautiful, dressed to the nines with nary a hair out of place. Every man had on a gorgeous outfit neatly tailored and pressed. Wiping the sweat which had dripped from my glasses on to the floor below I wondered why I was sweating so much. By now my shirt was drenched and almost fused to my suit jacket. My pants stuck to the bench when I got up.

After the ceremony, I quietly slipped outside for a few breaths of fresh air and to wring out my shirt. My new $125 Armani tie was drenched. Admiring the vista of the setting Sicilian sun gently sliding for the night behind Mt. Etna, a sense of calm came over me, my body temperature dropped and I began to feel more comfortable. Massimo came up to me. "Alfred" he said, "Every time you come from America it always takes you a few days to adjust. Our pace of life here is much slower than in the USA. If you let the Island embrace you, you will feel good in two seconds."

There is much more to life than running around like a chicken in the go-go-go existence that I lead in the States. I have to be reminded every now and again to slow down.

"Relax, Al," I said to myself, "you're home. Have a good time tonight". Straightening my tie, I buttoned by shirt and threw on my suit coat and almost felt and looked as dapper as any.

Looking at the road below, I waved to the pigeons as they walked by — too hot to fly, then jumped in the car, off to a fabulous reception and meal at the sixteenth century Spanish Castello San Marco, but that's another story.

7. Festa! Massimo's Birthday Party!

I had been looking forward to this all week. Massimo's surprise 44th birthday party that his wife Anna organized, and I wasn't disappointed, for sure.

Massimo's entire family was coming: his brother Alessandro and his family, his brother Michele and his family, his friend Marguerite and her husband, Massimo's mom Theresa, plus another couple that I did not know.

All told, there would be twenty of us.

A surprise party is different here in Sicily. No one hides or anything, they show up when they want. As a matter of fact, I was the only one who showed up at the appointed time: 7:00 PM.

The rest showed up at the normal time that people show up in Sicily, between 8 and 8:30.

I guess the surprise is that there isn't a surprise.

Massimo told me when I arrived: "Alfred, Anna told me that she planned a surprise party for me, so please help me get ready for it. "

I was surprised myself at this point, and said, "Sure!"

For the next hour, I played with Marzio, Massimo's son while everything was getting prepared. I love that kid and he loves me.

Tonight, he taught me the names of all the Disney characters in Italian and I taught him their names in English.

My favorite is "La Bella and il Bastardo"...Beauty and the Beast. I know a few guys with the same name in America, no relation though.

The dinner table was set very beautifully: a long elegant table with china and all the trimmings.

Tonight the cuisine was fish, as Anna had gone to the fish pier in Catania and bought fresh fish that was probably swimming around minding their own business earlier in the day.

I had helped Anna prepare the main course: a huge gutted whitefish that she had purchased and had placed on a huge flat pan.

Inside, she put slices of lemon, parsley and a little pepper (where it had been gutted), and packed the whole thing top and bottom with course sea salt: about ten pounds in all.

By the time the fish was prepped, there was a mound of salt, and a fish somewhere inside that mound. Popping that fish into the oven, she put the temp at 150 degrees Celsius and would come back in an hour when it was done.

All the relatives arrived, and the kissing began. One pecks on each cheek (always go to the right, or else you will bump heads).

The kids went off to play somewhere and the socializing began.

First we had a toast: Sans Bitters and Martini Bianco. Sans Bitters is a red soda made from bitters (we sell it at ATS) but here they put in Martini Bianco, which is a sweet aperitif (a kind of white wine actually). The result is a delicious drink.

Marguerite told me that it opens up the taste buds.

Everyone toasted Massimo saying "auguri" and then we sat to begin the festivities.

On the table set out in platters were the following as appetizers: mussels, oysters, a tiny shrimp dish made with shrimp, celery, a little parsley, salt and pepper, pan fried sardines (they were delicious), *mozzarella di bufala* and tomato (a soft cheese made from buffalo milk, also available in America), and one or two other small fish dishes that I did not recognize, but they tasted great.

Everyone scooped one or two items on their plate (for example, everyone took no more than two oysters, 4 or 5 mussles…just enough to taste everything.

An excellent white wine was served.

For the "secondo" (second course), a delicious sword fish, and noodle pasta was served in a delicious tomato sauce. Again, the portions were not huge. Only Americans serve big portions of pasta. I'd say there was the equivalent of about four forkfuls of pasta on each plate.

The fish that was encrusted with the sea salt was the main course, served with *patate al forno* (baked potatoes with olive oil, salt, pepper and parsley.)

Anna had filleted it and it was truly delicious. No bones, light and about ½ inch thick. Again everyone had a small serving, no more than two or three ounces.

The kids were playing in the playroom and were well behaved. The conversation lively and animated and everyone was enjoying themselves.

After dinner, we sang "Happy Birthday" in Italian and had a champagne toast. (Actually is was a white Sicilian *spumante*) and again everyone had just a small piece of cake.

The cake was a cream cake with boiled white pudding inside, topped with fresh strawberries, not a "cassata" cake but a very delicious cake.

Finally, fresh pineapple topped with fresh strawberries was served, along with "Amaro Averna," a regional after dinner aperitif that I truly love.

Even though the menu was a big one, people did not stuff themselves.

Honestly, I did not over eat at all, nor did anyone else. People eat much smaller portions thus the extensive variety of delicious fare.

Massimo has an insatiable sweet tooth despite the fact that he looks like Adonis. I bought him a SECOND birthday cake that he will polish off today for sure.

This was the third time that I have spent time here on Massimo's birthday. I have had Easter dinner with the family, Christmas dinner, and New Year's dinner here multiple times, and Massimo's family has become my adopted family.

Massimo's kids call me "Zio Alfredo" (uncle Alfred), so I really do have a family here.

All in all, a truly enjoyable and memorable night was had by all.

Many fish had died for us last night and by God it was greatly appreciated.

Chapter Ten

Food in General

Sicily is a fisherman's delight. I had a little villa in Pachino, right on the clear, tropical green-blue water on the Southeastern tip of the island where the Mediterranean and Ionian Seas meet. At night before I went to sleep, I used to throw my little fish net in the water by the rocks. When I awoke there was always fish in the net: a symbol of Sicily's plentiful bounty. Neighboring Pachino is the wonderful village of Porto Palo where I often dined at one of the best fish restaurants that I have ever encountered (Tokyo's fish restaurants are a close second, but we are talking Sicilian today, no?).

When I went to this particular restaurant, the owner who knew me (since I had brought many of my friends there over the years) brought us platter after platter of freshly grilled shrimp, prawn, calamari, tuna, whitefish and other delights too numerous to mention in presentations that would command a month's wages if served here in the States. In Sicily, fish is life and every Sicilian knows exactly where to buy his fresh fish, usually caught earlier that same day!

Although I highly recommend the plentiful fish in Sicily, the meat is not the same quality. Sicilian cattle are fed by land grazing, not the feed that American cattle are reared on and as a result the meat is a little tough and less tasty. Surprisingly, the same is true for the sausage. The USA has much better sausage, more flavorful. Anyone who has ever had an outdoor barbeque with sausage made from Butcher's Boy's Market in North Andover, MA or Borrelli's Deli in Methuen, MA or your own favorite butcher will realize that ours is a better quality meat. However, lamb and pork dishes in Sicily are great and if you like game dishes, Sicilian rabbit dishes are legendary.

Fruit and cereals abound all over the Island. Fresh peaches, strawberries, plums, watermelon, *nespole* (best described as a cross between an orange and a peach), *fichidindia* (cactus pear), pear, apricot, black mulberry, cantaloupe, plus many other great tasting fruits can be purchased on any street corner during the summer months. Of course, the blood oranges, lemons and regular oranges are the Island's signature fruits. And the figs taste like no others in the world. Simply put, Sicilian figs are heavenly.

Believe it or not, although most of Italy's pasta is now made in either Milan or Naples or in huge modern pasta factories on main-

66

land Italy, the Sicilians insist that pasta was first made in Sicily. (Of course, Poiatti Pasta from Mazara del Vallo compares favorably with anyone's pasta in the world.) As far back as 1200 AD there are references made in historical books to 'maccaruni,' the name originally given to pasta. As legend has it, William the Hermit was invited to a meal by a Sicilian nobleman who served him *cannelloni*. However, instead of being stuffed with ricotta cheese, the noodles were filled with pure earth. Undaunted, William blessed the food and by a miracle the earth became ricotta. This dish, the *cannelloni* of Catania, is stilled served in Catania, filled today, as they were then, with meat and cheese and served garnished with a great sauce! Most Sicilians eat their pasta with fish, anchovies, sardines, swordfish, clams, black squid ink (yummy!) and of course with olive oil and tomatoes.

Vegetables play an important role with pasta, too. *Pasta con le melanzane* (pasta with eggplant), is also known as *Pasta alla Norma* (after the composer Vincenzo Bellini) born in Catania in 1801. Pasta with every other conceivable vegetable thrown in makes eating pasta truly a gourmet experience! Quick! Put on the boiling water! I am getting hungry writing this!

Chapter Eleven

The New Place

1. Via Ulisse, No. 18.

Well, I signed the lease for the new place today! The lease runs for four years with a four-year option.

The condo is located in Aci Catena, overlooking both Acitrezza and Acicastello, two very famous places located on the Sicilian "Riviera Dei Ciclopi."

Acitrezza is the mythical place written about in Homer's "Ulysses." In this area, on Mt. Etna, Ulysses blinded Poliphemus who was holding prisoner in his cave. The *Riviera dei ciclopi* takes its name from the boulders Poliphermus hurled against the Greeks as they fled. The boulders landed in the sea off Acitrezza.

Today, Acitrezza is a popular beach area and tourist resort.

Acicastello is the site of a 10th century Norman castle. In the 11th century, the Normans invaded Sicily and defeated the Muslims who had occupied Sicily for two and a half centuries.

The castle is now a museum.

From my new balcony, I have a wonderful panoramic view of the castle and rocks of the Cyclops.

The place has three bedrooms but I will convert two of them into a suite for a couple as each is smaller than I wanted. Thus, I can rent it for a very low price.

Right now, rooms in a hotel nearby go for $200 a night. I think $500 a week for a couple is a bargain, and that is the price that I will charge. My dear friend, August from New York will take it for six or seven weeks next year, and I will rent it out maybe for another six weeks or so.

Now the fun begins. I need to find a mover, and get all the utilities turned on.

Thank God that Massimo and Maria will help.

I will return in December and stay there for the first time.

Now, I have to sort thru stuff here! Drat!

2. Sure Beats Mickey D's!

The day started off as a royal pain.

Massimo called me last night and told me that I had to get to the new condo by 8:00 AM in order to meet the guy from the gas company, as a last minute cancellation occurred and we had to move fast.

Getting utilities turned on in Sicily is always an adventure, so at 6:00 AM I dragged myself out of a fitful sleep and got ready to meet the guy. It was now or never.

The best way to get to the condo, I found, is driving on the shore road from Acireale. As I passed first Acireale and then Acitrezza, my spirits rose a bit. It was a beautiful Sicilian morning and the water was really glistening.

Off that main road is a sign for the President Park Hotel, where I turned right.

The condo is located in a small gated community up the hill (and I do mean a hill: the car was huffing and puffing) from the hotel. Via Ulisse, No. 18. The Corso di Oliva condos.

When I got there, of course, the automatic gate was closed and I didn't have a key yet.

I waited from 8:00 AM until 11:00 AM. I was standing under a beautiful olive tree at the entrance. The off-shore breeze swaying the palm trees. I didn't realize that palm trees make a whooshing noise when the wind passes. To kill time, I started to pick some olives. They were not for eating. They were past the time for picking. Still, as I split them open and smelled the fragrance, it was wonderful. I passed the time by rolling olives down the steep hill. Man, do olives roll when you throw them! Seriously.

However, doing absolutely nothing is why I came to Sicily. Throwing olives, letting the sun pound on you, imagining the Greek and Roman war vessels of two millennia past in the sea below. This is why I am here, I thought to myself.

Finally, the idiot arrived, three hours late, but at least he showed up. Two minutes later, the gas was switched on and I was on my way.

I stopped first by Despar, a mini-market to pick up bottled water and juice, then my stomach growled.

By this time it was noon and I was ready for lunch.

I knew exactly where to go. The *Tavola Calda* (Hot Table) in Valverde, one of my favorite lunch spots.

I eat pasta almost every day while in Sicily, but never at night. Today I had pasta 'al forno,' baked macaroni. The plate was so pretty that I felt that I had to pay for the view, so I threw a dollar bill at it.

It was unbelievable. "I can't wait to get hungry again," I thought to myself.

For the 'secondo' (second course), I had a cutlet, some baked potatoes cooked like my mom cooked then, in the oven, and some sweet peppers that had been roasted in oil.

An espresso finished off the spiritual event.

This meal is heaven to me. A simple meal that soothes the soul. This will be it for eating for the day though.

Usually at night I will have a salad or fruit and not another full meal. One meal a day, that's the secret. I have to fit into my bathing suit this summer. Right.

Completely satisfied and eager for tomorrow's lunch already, I headed back to the villa to do some work.

BYW, the lunch bill was 12 euros: about 15 dollars. That is what I usually spend, between 15 to 20 dollars a day here to eat. Very cheap.

Sure beats Mickey D's!

3. Cleaning House...Sicilian Style!

It's bad enough that I have to clean my condo in America. However, I have another to worry about: my condo in Sicily.

With visitors renting the place every so often, I want to make sure that the place is Spic and Span.

However, they don't sell Spic and Span there.

Here, I have a nifty Swifter that zips thru my floor in minutes.

There, I have a plastic bucket with this little thing on top to wring the water out.

Here, I just have to take that pad off the Velcro on the Swifter and throw the pad away.

There, I have to empty the bucket and wring the mop.

Here, I have Mr. Clean.

There, I have Mr. Muscolo.

You get the picture.

The most difficult part for me, however, is trying to figure out what product to buy at the supermarket.

The directions on the back of the aerosol spray cans, which even in America are so tiny that I need the Hubble telescope to read, and just as bad there, except that in addition to being tiny, they are also in Italian.

One time, thinking that I bought something like Lemon Pledge for my furniture, I sprayed a stain remover. Another time I put in a hard water de-calcifier in the washing machine instead of detergent. The worst thing I did, however, was spray talcum power all over the house thinking it was one of those odor eating aerosols.

It came out in a mist, but once it settled on everything, my place looked like the Winter Christmas Display at Macy's: white stuff all over the place.

I took me a week to clean it up.

Finally, I ended up hiring a man from Bangladesh who now comes in and cleans the whole place wonderfully.

He reads Italian too.

As bad as I make it seem, I actually enjoying cleaning my condo there. As I work up a sweat dusting, washing, and cleaning, I remind myself that I am in Sicily and that almost cancels everything out.

4. It Isn't Exactly Heaven...

Ever hear of the Stendhal Syndrome? That is the feeling that a person gets, often overwhelming, when returning from a vacation to a foreign land and then wants to sell everything in his home land and go back!

Frequently I get emails from people who have just returned from a trip to Italy or Sicily who are just dying to sell all their possessions and move to Rome, Florence, Tuscany, Sicily, just as long as it is in Italy.

Don't bother. As my grandfather used to say "Alfred, the grass is always greener on the other side of the pasture, but if you look closely, there are a lot of weeds there." Yup, I agree. I have been to Sicily so many times over the years and for extended periods too that I long ago realized that you better be prepared for MAJOR changes in your life if you want to keep you sanity. Consider the following as a recent example: I arrived here on Christmas day right in the middle of terrible weather. It had been raining non stop for three days. Sicilians can't handle rain. They think the end of the world is coming. The road infrastructure has horrible drainage, so enormous puddles develop everywhere. I felt like Noah driving a Fiat version of the Ark as I went to my villa! Arriving at the villa, I immediately turned the heat on. As I soon found out, it was one of the few things that worked over the next five days.

The first thing that went was the water. Seems that a pumping station nearby shorted out, and it took someone from the water company two days to flip a switch. In Italy, when you call to report a problem with the water, electricity, or telephone, they tell you that someone will be out in 48 hours, that is 48 hours of working time during the week. So, if something goes wrong on Friday, they don't look at it until 48 hours from Monday. Not repair it, mind you, just to look at it. It the water case, it was just a switch. We were lucky. I learned form past mistakes though. Fortunately, last summer I had a back up water tank with 1000 liters of water installed, so there was no problem. I remember when I was installing it, all the neighbors snickered. "Americans!" they said. "They want all the conveniences. Well, I was the one to snicker, I guess, as I was able to cook, shower, and flush the toilet! The next thing to go because of the storm was the electricity. Out came the candles. In three minutes the house was lit up. Since I had a gas heater installed, we had heat too. American ingenuity. The next day the phones went dead, and so did the lighting-quick ADSL broadband computer system that I had installed. Out came the American cell phone. Out too came the Italian cell phone that I had also purchased last summer, just in case. "What's next?" I thought, "Pestilence?"

Anyway, it took five days for the home phone and computer to be fixed. Nothing happens fast in Sicily. I had go to Acireale to do the computer work at the Internet Point all week. When it decided to open, that is. The woman who owns the internet point had relatives over, so she opened it up when she felt like it!

Next year I am getting one of those wireless systems that I can hook up to the cell phone in order to fire up the computer. If that doesn't work, I am going to string up a line with a can at both ends of the Atlantic! Yup, an American in Sicily. With all the conveniences of home. Just gotta keep on using that American ingenuity, though. Sicilian ingenuity sometimes just doesn't work!

5. Day Four....Solitude

Joe and Mary Ellen left this morning, and I had many things to do around the condo. Finally I got them done and decided that I needed some quiet time.

I decided that this condo is my favorite of the three previous places that I had. The layout is terrific and the view from the deck beyond belief.

I like being alone. I process things a little better, I think. This place is perfect for that.

As I said earlier, I had a very tough winter. The economy really has put my little company on the brink of extinction. Not only is that, but my personal life once again in shambles. Other than the rock-solid love and affection of my children and grandchildren (and believe me, it is enormous, their love always carries me through), I have some tough decisions to make.

While I truly am fond of Joe and his wife, I came to Sicily this time to heal and to think things through. Tough decisions, life altering decisions have to be made professionally and personally.

Robert Lewis Stevenson once said, "Sometimes you have to fight it out or perish. And if that is the case, why not here, where you stand?"

Thus, this trip is my stand, I think. However, intellect and not emotion must rule the day.

That's the problem with my legal training. Never a snap decision. Always examining a problem from all angles. Mulling an issue is my middle name.

I took a ride today to Acicastello: a small little fishing village a stone's throw from my place. It's claim to fame is a beautiful 11th century Norman castle that sits on the water's edge and guards the waterway. Surrounding the castle, on the land side is a fence where people can enjoy the spectacular view and enjoy themselves.

I leaned against the little fence there and gazed out at the Ionian sea, letting the warm ocean breeze embrace me. The sun was brilliant, the horizon endless.

Processing thoughts and emotions at this place is therapeutic, I think.

I stayed there for a couple hours alone.

There isn't a lot that I know about life, even at my old age, but one thing I do know is that I belong here. The constant tug of war between my responsibilities in America and the call of Sicily are very close to coming to and end.

The Dhalia Lama said, "the object of life is to be happy." Sicily and her people make me happy. Slowly, I am being drawn to a paradigm shift in life. Somehow I have to figure out a way to make the move here and reverse the trend of life.

However bad the economy is in America, it is much worse here. Thus the dilemma.

I think of my two grandfathers Alfio and Gaetano. Both arrived in America with less than twenty dollars in their pockets. I have forty dollars in mine right now. Why not?

Chapter Twelve

Holidays

1. The Legend(s) of San Valentino

Valentine's Day is the day which all the flower shops, Hallmark shops, and candy shops look forward to all year. Only the most dastardly ignore their loved ones on that day! It is practically a deportable offense to not send something or give something to your special someone on that day. But where did this day originate?

Well, we know for sure that Italy is the place. Then the fun starts. Many claim San Valentino as their own. Here is my favorite legend of the hundreds that are out there:

In the third century AD, The Emperor Claudius II ruled Rome. Feeling threatened by the emerging Christian religion, he tried to stamp it out, considering it to be a threat to the state. Christians were persecuted, killed, imprisoned, thrown to the lions. You get the picture.

In Umbria, a priest named Valentino was named bishop in the town of Terni, which was also a Roman garrison. One day, a young boy and girl visited him, and he gave them a flower from his garden, they fell in love and got married. Soon, everyone wanted a flower from Valentino for good luck, and he eventually put aside one day dedicated to the state of matrimony.

Claudius' governor in Terni evidently didn't appreciate this. Customs like getting married were forbidden if you were in the Roman Legion. It ruined the *esprit de corps*, Romans believed. (Hmmm, might have a point there!) Anyway, Valentine was caught marrying people, including a couple of Roman Legionnaires. He was imprisoned, naturally.

In jail, Valentino left a note to the daughter of his jailer shortly before his death and signed it "Your Valentine" He was beheaded or crucified and several years later he was named a saint.

The town of Terni embraced Valentino, but not until the 17th century, almost 1300 years later. He was named patron saint of the city in 1640, and a huge annual festival is now held every year. Today, Terni is known as "Città di San Valentino, città d'amore," (city of San Valentino, city of love.) Additionally, major awards are presented annually to people who have accomplished the most to promote peace and love in the world. This year, Kerry Kennedy, the daughter of Robert F. Kennedy, who runs the Robert F. Kennedy Center For Human Rights and also the RFK Foundation in Europe will be honored as this year's winner.

Sicilians, of course, have a slightly different view.

First of all, with some Sicilian men, Valentine's Day is every day in Sicily, as long as no gifts need to be purchased. Surprisingly, Sicilian men aren't generally romantic in the gift-giving sense. They talk a good game with their pals at the local espresso shop, but when push comes to shove, only infrequently do they show up with candy, flowers or a card.

"What for?" someone once said to me. "We're married!"

Yikes! I could never get away with that!

Young Sicilian lovers do have a nice tradition though (note I specified "young". Evidently the view changes over time). Many shops feature small baskets with beautiful china and candy that young lovers buy for their sweethearts.

Saint Valentine was on to something: love is always the eternal answer. Somehow, however, once U.S. marketers got wind of Valentine, the Greek and Roman symbol, Cupid, got involved, and Valentine's Day developed into an important sales day throughout the country. Today my local newspaper is filled with many Valentine's Specials from car dealers!

Oh well! Thank God there isn't a patron saint in Italy for groundhogs!

2: Easter Essay

When I was a young boy, Lent was one of my favorite times of the year.

As a good Catholic boy (back in those days at least), I loved the seriousness of that forty day period leading up to Easter.

At Sacred Heart School For Boys in Andover, MA that I attended grades four to eight, Lent meant going to chapel every single Friday instead of the normal once a month First Friday ritual.

I got shipped to Sacred Heart by my parents because the nuns (allegedly) couldn't handle me at Holy Rosary School in Lawrence, Massachusetts, and the Brothers of the Sacred Heart had a certain "keen disciplinary approach," shall we say.

More than once (usually, a day) the brothers there got and kept the attention of both me and my backside (if you know what I mean).

Those guys were big, tough and knew all about the "swift hand of retribution" educational philosophy.

However, I loved chapel. The chapel was always warm and comforting; incense always filled the air, as did the Latin hymns that we sang. The sound of some Latin songs still reverberate in my head whenever I smell a whiff of incense. The sun always seemed to glisten in through the beautiful stained glass windows of that chapel, and I always loved that place.

Fridays, especially Good Friday, were always solemn occasions back then. As I result, a certain religious fervor was ingrained in me that last to this day.

On the week leading up to Easter, we spent all day, every day in Chapel. All the gospels of all four evangelists were read every day, and we really agonized over the passion of Christ. Those brothers certainly knew how to drill home to a youngster the pain and passion of Jesus, for sure. However, for me at least, as I got older and went on to high school, college, law school, raised kids etc., the general tenor of this period took a back seat to the goings on of my daily life.

I think I needed a refresher course on spirituality.

It is with that background that I went to Sicily to capture the mindset of the Sicilians during this period of the liturgy. There, the Lent period is a contrast between the good and bad; the forces of evil versus the forces of goodness; lightness versus darkness; the Devil versus God.

On Good Friday, in Sicily, it doesn't get any darker or sadder anywhere. Usually churches are filled with people, just like it used to be here when I was a kid.

I had the honor of witnessing first hand over the years the procession of the faithful at Enna, where on Good Friday the body of Jesus is paraded up and down the streets and the "vara" is pulled by hundreds of hooded men and boys in a sorrowful manner.

The music that is played by the saddened band haunts the soul. Every note, every song is filled with sadness. Tears welled in my eyes and a lump gathered in my throat as the dead Jesus passed me. For a nanosecond there, I was transported back in time to the Chapel at Sacred Heart and the emotions of a young boy were unearthed, re-lived.

In Enna, hooded penitents wear those garments because they believe that they are sinners and that they are unworthy to be looked on by God. For Sicilians, on that day, the forces of darkness have triumphed. Noted processions also take place in Marsala and San Fratello. All three are haunting examples of the solemn mood which envelops Sicily that day.

On Easter Sunday, however, joy reins supreme all over the Island. A different statue is paraded through Enna. The statue of the raised Jesus. People cheer, they dance. The forces of goodness triumph. The Devil is defeated, lightness dominates.

Funny, I don't see many Easter bunnies there. I see no hopping around. I do see the traditional Easter breads, the egg baked into the beautiful cookie, flowers.

I see people dressed in their finest going to Church Easter morning. I see them visiting departed ones at the cemetery. I see little kids scrubbed clean with wonderful Easter outfits, just like it used to be here in the States long ago.

So to me, the Lent-Easter period is frozen in time in Sicily. If I want to re-live my childhood memories of this period, this is where I go. Everything is still intact.

Here is what I know: if you ever have the opportunity to make the pilgrimage to Enna for Holy Week, do it. It will revive and nourish your soul. That is a fact.

3. Sicilian Easter Traditions Essay Two

In the last newsletter, I wrote about Carnival in Sicily: the last big "party" that the Island has before Lent, which is the period of time between Ash Wednesday and Easter Sunday, when all of Christendom remembers the Passion, Death and Resurrection of Jesus Christ. Far and away, this period of time is the holiest time in Sicily, surpassing even the Christmas season in terms of religious fervor. The first noticeable contrast between the US and Sicily is that except for a few "Americanized" areas, the Easter Bunny cannot be found. As Sicily is nearly completely Roman Catholic (other religious groups have a presence, but fundamentally, Sicily remains overwhelmingly Catholic), the Passion and Death of Jesus Christ is played and replayed in nearly every village town and city leading up to Easter.

The Easter traditions that have developed in Sicily are very different depending on the local traditions. Broadly speaking, the observance of Pasqua in Sicily focuses on two very different themes. In Palermo, San Fratello, and Adrano, for instance, the forces of Darkness, symbolized by Lucifer and scary men dressed in horrid iron masks and other costumes, symbolize the capture of souls after the death of Jesus Christ and the attempted disruption of religious activity. These allegories cease with the start of the Easter procession which displays Jesus or the Madonna defeating Lucifer and company and causing them to fall silent and flee. Palermo's "Dance of the Devils," San Fratello's "The Devils of San Fratello" and "The Diavolta" in Adrano (which is a religious folk drama held in the town square) all celebrate the banishment of the forces of evil by the forces of goodness, of the victory of the forces of light over the forces of darkness.

A short essay like mine really does not do justice to the events of Easter in Sicily. If you are a religious person then, Sicily (or anywhere in Italy for that matter) is the place for you during this holiest of times. As a child growing up in Lawrence, Massachusetts and living among first generation Sicilian immigrants, Easter was always my favorite time of the year. I can still see my late grandfather Alfio Zappalà sitting by the couch on Palm Sunday making a crucifix from the Palm given to him at church that day. As a matter of fact, the last palm crucifix that he made (in 1974 shortly before his death), still hangs in my bedroom, where it has been for the last 30 years.

4. "Ferragosto"

On August 15th every year, Italy celebrates "Ferragosto" (from the Roman feast to Diana – Feriae Augusti – Fairs of August) is a national holiday commemorating the fact that the 15th of the month is the middle of August.

No kidding.

The entire country shuts down and moves from the north to the south (usually Sicily) for one week. Sicily is flooded with Italians on holiday. Right on cue, the airlines usually have a one day strike protesting something inane and as a result flights are delayed, bags are lost and havoc is the result.

I remember once I flew in on August 15th. When I arrived in Sicily, my bags were lost. This was before I had my place there and didn't have back up clothes. After three days of no change of clothes, I was getting desperate.

I decided to buy myself a new wardrobe. I remember going into the discount store in Misterbianco and heading straight to the underwear section. I wear boxers, size XXL, not those tiny pouch things. I asked the clerk for boxers. She looked at me like I had grown a second head. "Why?" she asked. Why? I nearly killed her. Anyway, after rummaging through the back bins, she found a pack of four underwear size XXL all wrapped up in cellophane. I kissed her, bought my four treasures, and headed to the hotel where I was planning a memorial burning ceremony commemorating the valiant way that my American made undies had so heroically performed. These undies deserve to be in the Undie Hall Of Fame I thought as I lit the match in my hotel wastebasket. I even remember taking a small bottle of champagne from the mini bar sparing no expense that morning.

After saying a few words and watching the heroic Eddie Bauer blue-checked boxers ascend into boxer heaven, I marched into the shower, scrubbing my body in eager anticipation of my new XXL white boxers still cellophane-encased. You can imagine my horror when the new white boxers didn't even make it over my knees. No way. These XXLs were the American equivalent of a men's medium here in the states. I struggled in that hotel room pulling those things up, and nearly threw my back out doing so. My belly went right up to my shoulders and for a few minutes I resembled Arnold Schwarzenegger there . . . until they ripped apart.

After getting the circulation in my lower body back, and after peeling those skivvies off shred by shred, the doorman delivered my bags from the US. Ever see a grown man cry unpacking his bags?

Anyway, a lesson learned. Today, when I travel, in my carry-on is my passport, my book, my medicine and a new pair of Eddie Bauer boxers, just in case!

5: A Sicilian Thanksgiving Story!

I am often asked about Thanksgiving in Italy.

Of course, Thanksgiving is an American holiday, so Thanksgiving is just a regular day in Sicily.

A few years ago, I decided to take all my kids and their beaus to Sicily with me for Thanksgiving, a family road trip so to speak.

My daughter Jen, her fiancée JR (now her husband), my daughter Catie (a cool rock and roll singer now), and my son Matt (a government lawyer) and his then fiancée (now wife) Lindsay boarded a plane and headed to the villa to spend the holiday together.

Six of us on a Sicilian Thanksgiving road-trip.

We arrived a few days before Thanksgiving, and the first thing we did was hit the markets for all the Thanksgiving fixings.

We bought fresh vegetable, yummy potatoes, great fruit, nuts, cheese, you name it: everything necessary for a delectable Thanksgiving meal.

One problem though.

Turkeys are not sold in Sicily.

Only thing available: scrawny chickens that looked like they had been run to death, almost no meat on those guys.

So here we were, a shopping carts full of all sorts of goodies, with no main dish!

In desperation, when we got back to the villa, I paid a visit to my neighbor, a US serviceman on duty at the nearby US Naval Station in Catania.

After explaining the situation to him, he told me that he could get a turkey for me at the base supermarket, which had American grocery items on sale.

We were all excited.

Until he came home with that bird.

It was a 20 ponder, all right, except it was frozen solid.

Rock solid.

As Catie said: "Way, way solid! Nitrogen solid."

Never had I seen anything so well frozen. This thing could have lasted frozen for a week in the Sahara Desert, I thought.

For 2 days, that bird lay in the sink….and we watched it slowly, very slowly thaw out, inch by inch, hour by hour.

We had never seen such a "freeze job" like that before!

Finally, the thing was "ready to go."

So we thought.

In horror, we realized that there was no way that such a big bird would fit into our small Italian oven!

Yikes!

After much debate as to what to do, the decision was to cut up that thawed bird raw and cook the pieces.

That is when the idea hit: I remembered that my grandmother used to cook her chickens and baste then with a mixture of rosemary, a little salt and pepper and olive oil.

That is exactly what we did: we covered that bird with a gorgeous mixture of that splendid concoction and threw the potatoes in the cooking pan too.

The results were wonderful.

A perfectly cooked bird, succulent to the taste and the hit of the show!

We ended up having a wonderful "Sicilian" Thanksgiving with turkey cooked "Sicilian" style!

Best bird we ever ate and a topic of fond remembrance every year since. Happy Thanksgiving!

6. Christmas

As I get older, I cannot help to think about days gone by.

This time of year, I think about the holidays back when I was a young boy, then a young man, then as a young adult.

We accumulate so many memories as we go thru life though that is hard to reflect on only one feeling.

While I treasure my two granddaughters and grandsons today, I will see them and celebrate Christmas Eve with them before I depart to Sicily on Christmas Day, mostly at this time of year, I think about my loved ones who are not here with me.

And, as I plod on through the years, that list gets longer and longer, it seems.

It will be 12 years since my dad passed come this December 29. Even though the years have flown by since that day, I think of him often. For sure, every holiday now carries a twinge of sadness. I think of the Christmas displays in the nursing home those last days, and remember how I struggled emotionally back then.

I remember, too, the feelings of anticipation that I had as a young boy in my childhood house: visions of my grandfather and grandmother, now departed, still float in my head, along with the sights and sounds of gaiety that filled the house of aunts, uncles, cousins, friends long departed. Geez! Life can be tough sometimes.

I console myself with the young today. My children, grand kids, nieces and nephews. I think of my uncle Tom, always amazing the children with tricks and that twinkle in his eye.

If I could have a wish, however, just a single wish, it would be that have every loved one, past and present, could be together just more time for Christmas.

In mind, in my soul, and in my heart this is what happens to me every Holiday season: the memories of happiness from bygone years with so many people who truly loved me as I loved them. Those memories are ingrained forever in my mind's eye.

I know they are with me though. If I look real hard, I can see them everywhere, in the eyes of my friends and family, in the scents and textures of a Christmas song, in the fond remembrance of a favorite old movie, maybe a Bing Crosby or Fred Astaire one.

This I know: there are still plenty of things around here that link me to them. It's just that I have to keep looking harder and harder every year, I think.

I bet you feel the same.

7. On Christmas Again

It's Christmas Time in Italy! Another Christmas.

Walking down the streets of Rome or Taormina during the Christmas season is an experience that I hope you can someday enjoy.

While there is something special about the wintry wonderland of New England during the Christmas season, enjoying a truly "Italian" Christmas experience, which is much different in flavor, texture, and ambiance from "ours" in America is something unforgettable.

Almost everything in Italy and Sicily over the holidays revolves around the birth of the infant Jesus, and while Santa Clause is now too all over the place there, the hysteria of "Santa" isn't as profound as it is here.

First of all, Santa's name in Italy is "Babbo Natale", and he doesn't have Rudolph to help him like he does here! Then there is also the Legend of "La Befana" (the Befana legend is based on the story of a woman who looks like a Halloween witch who refused go with the Magi to see the newborn Jesus because she was too busy. Now she wanders the earth looking for Him to give him a present). Even that story, though, has religious implications.

Saint Francis of Assisi was the first to ask permission of the Pope to display a Nativity scene. In those days, statues were considered a form of idol worship and were not allowed. However, the pope relented and Francis put up the first manger.

Today, Italian Nativity scenes are light years ahead of ours in terms of beauty and care of construction. Simply walk to any piazza in Rome or Sicily and you will be stunned with the exacting detail of each Nativity manger that you come across. Most family nativities are generational, that is, you will see pieces decades old, passed down from father to son.

Surprisingly, Christmas trees, usually from Germany are abundant even in Sicily. Usually they are much smaller in size, however, and do not appear as "full" as those we have.

There is no such thing as mistletoe either.

To me, the sight and sound of seeing and listening to a group of Italian school children last year sing "Silent Night" in Italian still resonates in my ears. Then, I was fortunate to witness these kids sing Christmas carols on Christmas Night in Rome, and my heart was truly touched.

I swear I saw an angel or two singing with them in the group!

Anyway, Christmas anyplace is great here, there, on the moon. The most important thing is the "spirit" of the occasion, a spirit that I wish all of mankind could carry all year long!

On Christmas Day I will be in Sicily again. Maybe I will see those angels too.

Buon Natale!

8: Christmas Time Essay Three

Bittersweet Memory

Days gone by. (*Alfred this is identiccal with the text of two stories before! I am deleting it.*

While I treasure my two granddaughters today….yesterday they came to the house to wish me an early Merry Christmas. At this time of year I cannot help but think of members of my family who no longer with us.

It will be 11 years since my dad passed come this December 29. Even though the years have flown by since that day, I think of him often. For sure, every holiday now carries a twinge of sadness. I think of the Christmas displays in the nursing home those last days and remember how I struggled emotionally back then.

I remember too the feelings of anticipation that I had as a young boy in my childhood house: visions of my grandfather and grandmother, now departed still float in my head, along with the sights and sounds of gaiety that filled the house of departed aunts and uncles.

I can still smell the scents of a busy kitchen filled with my mother, grandmother, and aunts hurrying to and fro; the "stocco" cooking on the stove with its pungent odor that filled every nook and cranny of the house, the ever present baked-eggplant, the chicken soup (we never called it Italian Wedding Soup, though), plus all the traditional fish dishes.

I remember playing "scopa" and "sette e menzu"...two Sicilian card games my grandfather taught me and later on in life the cut throat game of 45's (a local game played in the Merrimack Valley in Massachusetts and also in parts of Canada).

Geez, life flies by.

9: Christmas Time Essay Four

Holiday Vocabulary Primer

Here is a basic primer of Holiday words and phrases that everyone can use!

General Words:

Buon Natale! - Merry Christmas!

Babbo Natale - Santa

il regalo di Natale - Christmas Presents

la Befana – The old witch that gives presents on the Twelfth Night

il Capodanno- New Year's Day

il canto di Natale- Christmas carol

la vigilia di Natale- Christmas Eve

Religious Words/Themes

Gesù Bambio – Infant Jesus

I Re Magi- The Three Magi

il presepio – A Nativity creche

La festa di Santo Stefano- Saint Stephen's day

La festa dell'Epifania- The Feast of the Epiphany

10. Christmas Time Essay Five (Alfred, this is something you said before! I am deleting it!)

.

11. Sicilian New Year's Feast

Sometimes I think Massimo wants to kill me. I keep him pretty busy doing things for me, big things too like coordinating the moving for my old place to the new place, making arrangements for (some) of the utilities to work, basically a million things this guy does for me.

That is why I love him and his wife Anna like family.

They are family.

In my new place, which is gorgeous, the heater blew again. I haven't had heat or hot water for a few days. Finally, a brand new one will be installed tomorrow. Anyway, yesterday, I went to Massimo's for New Year's Day dinner with Massimo and his family.

Imagine the best home cooked meal that you ever had. Imagine everything being cooked from scratch.

Fresh tortellini with a wonderful sauce, delicious appetizers too numerous to mention, wonderful cutlets, oven baked potatoes, special olive oil brought out only for the best occasions, great desserts, great wine: simply a wonderful day with Massimo and his family.

His three year old Marzio is growing like a weed. Tall and with big brown eyes, this kid will be a lady killer some day. The newest arrival, Carola, almost one year old, was an angel.

Massimo's mother, Theresa from Malta and who speaks fluent English, gave me a lecture on why Barrack Obama was the best thing to happen since sliced bread.

I am a Republican, and that's still a touchy subject though!

However, Massimo has transformed his "tavernetta" (fully finished basement) into a mini Sicilian Disney World for the kids: wall to wall Mickeys, Plutos, Cinderellas, every single Disney character now festoons the tavernetta.

A kids' paradise like I have never seen!

I spent three wonderful, family hours with the family, my fifth straight. New Year's Day there and being with Massimo and the family is now a tradition for me.

I went back to my place a happy guy, cold but happy, feeling very lucky that I have such a wonderful friend, my best friend actually, who does everything for me and my America family.

Thank you Massimo and Anna!

Now, where are the blankets?

12. *Nonno's* Story

Early January means two things in Sicily: huge sales in the stores and the Feast of La Befana.

Sicilian women are nuts over sales and I laughed as I witnessed many a tug of war over items the last two weeks there. As I wasn't familiar with the Befana tradition, I decided to learn a bit about it.

This year I decided to buy Befana doll or something for my three year old granddaughter Rose Catherine, as I thought it was about time that I explained the tradition to her.

It was easy to find a Befana doll: they are all over the place. However, I didn't want a scary one. Really, a Befana doll looks to me like a re-cycled Halloween witch doll. Befana is, after all, an old woman who looks like one. I searched for a happy witch Befana and found one. The doll had a smile on her face, was sitting on a broom, but was carrying a bag of goodies. For those of you who don't know the Befana was an old woman who refused to go with the Three Magi to adore the infant Jesus because she was too busy cleaning her house. Later on, she realized the mistake that she made and she set off for Bethlehem on her own searching for baby Jesus. Alas, by that time, the Magi had left and she couldn't find Him. The legend has it that she is still searching for the infant Jesus with a bag of gifts for him, hence the tradition.

To me, it sounds like a marketing gimmick. However, in Sicily, the kids go nuts over this day. There are Befana dolls, T-shirts, coloring books, games, you name it. And every store has a neat display. After selecting a nice Befana, I tucked it into my bags and returned to America. After recovering my luggage from Northwest who lost it (yes, they lost it), I headed to my daughter Jen's house to present Befana to Rosie.

My granddaughter Rosie really is the light of my life. She is a special person with a spirit that is just remarkable. We have developed a close grandfather-granddaughter bond that I still am processing. This little child has re-awakened feeling of love that this old geezer thought were long lost.

Anyway, I went through a whole rigmarole with her. I sat her on my lap, unwrapped the present, told her a long and beautiful story of the legend of Befana, then presented it to her.

She stared at the dolls for a while. Then she said "Nonno, you're fooling me. This is a witch. It's not Halloween!"

I swear, It took me an hour to explain to Rosie that this was a good witch. Finally, I concocted a story and told her that Befana was a sister of the Halloween witch, and she suspiciously accepted the explanation. By the next day, she had processed the whole thing and Befana is now part of Rosie's life.

I feel good about this. Most Sicilian-American kids know little about this tradition. Same with Italian-American kids.

When my son Matt's daughter Noey, who is a year and a half hits two and a half next year, I will get her a Befana doll and try to explain the story to her. However, my son Matt is a lawyer. I hope that hasn't yet rubbed off on her. It will make the story a tad harder for her to accept, I think! Anyway, Happy La Befana Day!

Chapter Thirteen

Sunday Dinner

When I was kid, Sunday dinners were a big deal. In my mind's eye I still see my mom, dad, grandfather (white shirt and tie), grandmother, and a few aunts and uncles sitting around our dinner table with a mountain of food., talking and eating at the same time. I think of the smells and sounds of my childhood. When I think of those bygone days, I wonder what happened. How did I get away from that family day?

As I got older, it seems, life took me in a different direction. Those dinners became less frequent until they finally stopped. Now, Sundays in America is usually throwing something on the grill at half time of a football game. Sunday dinners, it seems, gave way to the big screen TV and the NFL.

Not here in Sicily.

Sunday is still family day. A day where the grandparents come over and share a meal.

This morning I got up and after cleaning up a bit (gosh, it seems that I always cleaning up), I headed to the bakery and bought three pistachio cannoli, three ricotta cannoli, three boiled cream cannoli, two "baba", and a couple of other delights and headed to Massimo's house to join him and his family for Sunday dinner. As he has done faithfully for the past eight years, Massimo had to pick up his mom in Catania and then head to Viagrande to pick up his mother in law Angels. One is 79, the other 82. At the house cooking Sunday dinner was Anna and the two kids, Marzio and Carola.

When I got there, Massimo hadn't yet returned (I forgot that in Sicilian time 12:30 really means 1 PM), so I played with the kids a bit. I taught Marzio how to count to 10 in English and then we made a birthday card for Massimo because next Friday is his 45th birthday (same day as my son Matt).

Anna was busy preparing the quintessential Sunday dinner: *Pasta alla Norma* (pasta with eggplant and a sweet basil sauce) and also those things that are meat on the outside and have pieces of egg and other stuff in the inside and are tied together with a string Sitting around the table and with me in halting Italian, we talked about the troubles the Pope was having in Rome with the sex scandal, the European economy, and other interesting stuff that I don't

usually talk about on Sundays. The kids, surprisingly, were well behaved. I had promised them that I would teach them more English
after dinner if they behaved, and both had halos over their head.
Anna made *patate al forno* (potatoes, rosemary, olive oil baked just
the way I like them) and also some fresh bread and an "insalata mista"
was there too. A simple Sicilian meal. A meal that I sure was served
today in many Sicilian households. After dinner, I played with the
kids some more, then said my goodbyes until next Sunday when I
will mooch yet another meal. I was thinking about that meal all day:
it wasn't anything special, I've eaten it many times, but at the same
time it was special. It was, to me, reminiscent of my own childhood
and of a day that I used to have. Gosh, I miss those days. A lot.

Chapter Fourteen

Speaking Da Lingo!

Past tense, future tense, singular, plural, masculine, feminine, who can possibly learn Italian at my old age?

My problem is that I was brought up in a bi-lingual household that spoke "Sicilian," old "Sicilian" from 100 years ago when both sets of my grandparents arrived in the states from Sicily.

Unless people in Sicily are rfeally OLD, I sound like Jed Clampett from the Beverly Hillbillies when I talk "Italian."

Geez.

I like speaking "Sicilian". Trouble is, very few in Sicily speak the lingo every day. Youngsters speak Sicilian at family gatherings when all the old timers are there, but then speak Italian every day.

Not that's it a dying language (there is a strong movement afoot there to teach Sicilian again in schools), it's just that I guess I am caught up in the past and not the future.

Tough.

I will continue to speak my form of Sicilian, and when people there ask me, I will tell them:

SONO SICILIANO. Wait a minute: SUGNU SICILIANU!

There, that's better!

Chapter Fifteen

1. Everyday Life

After being here almost two weeks now, yesterday was the day to police the house a bit and put things back into a semblance of order. The first order of business was washing the floors on the first level. Unlike America where I have hardwood floors, here I have marble floors, which means washing by mop and pail. I have this plastic bucket with this thing on the top of it where you put the mop and twist out the water. The floor detergent I have has a wonderful fragrance to it and really does a good job. It is important to keep the floors very clean in the hot weather or else the ants will quickly establish themselves and become a nuisance. Little morsels of food left there must be swept daily, which typically I am very good about doing.

In any case, in about an hour, the floors were sparkling. I tackled the laundry next. I have a pretty decent European model which tumbles the clothes clean as opposed to the American models which has that agitator in the middle. Last year I was so impressed with how clean my stuff came out that I bought a great model at Best Buy in America and actually look forward to doing the laundry there. The clothes come out almost like new, with little discoloration or shrinkage. Plus, I need only a little detergent and the stuff I have also has a wonderful scent.

Here, I do not have a dryer. I have a portable plastic thing that I put on my deck and hang the clothes to dry in the sun. Again, they look and feel completely different than when I stick things in my dryer back home.

Three loads later (the machine is not a big one), my boxers were clean, my towels spiffy, and my "house clothes" all clean. Being a creature of habit, I am one of those people who take jeans and shirts to the dry cleaner. Here, my jeans always have a razor crease. My shirts are well pressed, although I use no starch here. I will drop off stuff at the dry cleaner later this afternoon.

Next I tackled the woodwork, which can be tricky. Here, the brand names are different than those back home and I can't read the small Italian print on the bottles. Last year I nearly ruined everything I had because I sprayed bug killer on the woodwork thinking it was Lemon Pledge. Today, using the right stuff, I cleaned all the woodwork. In three hours, the whole house was again clean, Sicilian style.

This morning is shopping day. I will zip to the panficio (bakery) to get fresh bread. Then to the green grocer to pick up my fruits and veggies. I made a killer sauce a couple days ago with fresh calamari, passata and basil that was killer. I have had a desire for "Cozze,"mussels. So I think I will pick some up and make some for dinner. Tonight I will head back to Naxos and hang at Roberto's place and see the sights a bit. Everyday life here is similar to back home but at a much slower pace. Here, I don't care about bills so much. I guess I will always have bills to pay. I am not running at 100 MPH like back home. Here, I slow down to 30MPH and try to relax a bit. I love my coffee here too. Tomorrow I will start my serious writing and for the next seven days I will write a business plan and try to figure out how to make a living here in eighteen months when I will return here permanently. I have a plan and now I need to reduce it to paper.

2. The Lido of the *Ciclopi*

Not wanting to drive twenty miles every day in order to hang on my favorite beach (I am on a budget this time), yet wanting to get some sun and enjoy the local scenery, I decided to scout out a few of the local lidos. A lido is a beach. You pay an admission and it usually has a beach-side restaurant or two, a bunch of cabanas where you can change into your "costume di bagno", and chairs or recliners with an umbrellas. The cost is usually around 10 euro (about $13.00) for the day.

The one I selected, after visiting several was the Lido dei Ciclopi in Acitrezza and I wonder why I didn't find this wonderful place sooner.

I went in and asked to see the manager. The place formally opens on Thursday, so it was closed. However, he gave me a tour of the place and I was very impressed.

Over the sea, with the Rocks of Acitrezza as a backdrop, there were three huge wood and metal decks, each about forty yards square, and on each deck there were about 100 umbrellas and beach chairs. At the end of each deck was a ramp or ladder where you lowered yourself into the sea.

Many of the beaches in Sicily have rocks on them. I usually hate swimming there as I always seems to hurt my feet. Here, it doesn't look to be a problem. Simply lower yourself into about five feet of water and swim away.

Plus, there is a beautiful swimming pool too.

The drive from my condo took five minutes so I do not have to worry about traffic, burning expensive gas ($6.00 a gallon), tolls, public parking, just pay 10 euro and enjoy the sights.

Anyway, tomorrow the weather will be hot, so I have my baggy swimming suit ready, my white fedora with black trim, and some 60 sun block all packed and ready to go.

Ten euros.

That is the cost of a latté and muffin at Starbucks.

3. You've Come a Long Way, Baby!

When thinking of Sicilian women, some envision little old ladies dressed in black from head to foot, wrapped in shawls and stockings knotted at the knees.

Truth be told, the description fits both of my late beloved grandmothers, but boy, oh boy, have women in Sicily come a long way, baby!

Due to the highly conservative Saracen (Arab) occupation that occurred in Sicily in the 10th and 11th centuries, Sicilian society adopted many of the customs and traditions of the occupiers. As a result, the Arab culture influenced the perception of women in Sicilian society.

First and foremost, the male was the absolute ruler of the household. As a matter of fact, at dinner time he ate first, the best food, prior to the women or children. Women in the 10th and 11th centuries donned a burka style dress, very similar to garments that we see on television today worn by Muslim women all over the world. The woman was precious to the man and had to be hidden lest she be stolen. And the feminine figure was never to be flaunted so as not to tempt any man. Thus the shawl and burka. Black was (and still is) the color of mourning in Sicily and since men often died long before their spouses due to the harsh and unforgiving living conditions, my grandmothers' garb has been traditional. Boy have things changed!

Today's Sicilian woman is a modern woman, many hold high government positions or work in other areas to help support the family. Those black-garbed images are now a distant memory, even grandmothers are stylishly dressed!

High fashion abounds in Sicily. Palermo's Via Roma and Catania's Corso Sicilia are lined with every designer shop imaginable. Taormina, the Pearl of Europe, hosts the European jet set lifestyle. Siracusa, Messina, Trapani and Agrigento also exhibit the high fashion of the modern Sicilian era, and one only has to visit any swimming area to realize that Sicily now is firmly entrenched in the 21st century. Last week one of my business partners, Donnamarie Pignone, who travels to Sicily extensively, dropped by the Lawrence shop with a beautiful young Sicilian woman named Agata. Agata teaches at the Babilonia Center for Italian Language and Culture in Taormina, but has been teaching Italian this academic year as a visiting professor at Elon University in North Carolina. Her English was flawless, her dress impeccable, her spirit irrepressible.

Agata informed me that women now occupy over 50% of all university faculty positions in Sicily and that they have become a vital component of the Sicilian economy. Young girls are taught about equality, opportunity, and the dignity of women in general, and it has been that way for the last several decades.

I was happy to learn that Sicilian women, (and believe me, I think Sicilian women are absolutely the most beautiful creatures on this earth), have thrown off the yoke of oppression and now stand with their male counterparts, shoulder to shoulder as equals.

Another reason to be proud of our heritage!

4. Whale Watching Sicilian Style.

Summertime is beach time in New England and it's no different for Sicilians.

Nothing beats the hot weather better than a day at the beach, and today I will tell you about my favorite Sicilian beach.

First, choosing the right swim wear is important. Being a big guy, I have always been careful when I buy a bathing suit to get one that, well...doesn't make me look like a whale!

Years ago I discovered just the right suit at the famous mail order house Eddie Bauer and I always make sure that this loose fitting, baggy suit is in my bag. Loose fitting, baggy, just above the knees: a perfect suit for a whale! Of course, at the beach in Sicily I stick out like a sore thumb, since all Sicilian men wear these yucky skimpy little pouch-type skin tight bathing suits, even big, fat guys like me!

Right off the bat I must look like a dork to Sicilians, but there is only so far that I will go to "look like the locals" and skimpy suits is that line! My girlfriend, Olga, on the other hand, doesn't have this problem. Having a nice figure, she fits right in and always wears the latest European style of suit. You can imagine how the two of us look at the beach: the beautiful European-looking goddess followed by the frumpy looking, fat guy in the baggy bathing suit. What a pair!

Our favorite beach is called "Lido La Romantica" in Giardini Naxos. For 8 euros (about $10.00) you get access to a private area complete with lounge chairs, umbrella, showers: the whole nine yards. The sand is soft, white and rock-free, and with the backdrop of Taormina looming in the background on one side with Mt. Etna on the other, I doubt a finer beach exists anywhere.

Settling in my chair, I observe the people around me. They are from all over Europe: Holland, Germany and Russia especially. A few Americans are here and there.

It is very easy to tell who is from where too. The American women wear bathing tops; the rest don't. Surprisingly, Sicilian women always wear tops and it is frowned upon to do otherwise!

As I dip my feet in the water, I notice it is clean. I can see little fish swimming around, and the water is warm, too, not like the New England shore beaches that I usually frequent. Diving in, it take me about 30 seconds to "get used" to the water. Heaven!

After a nice swim, I join Olga, who is sunbathing. The goddess and the frump. "I can't go in, Alfred; it will ruin my hair," she says. "Hmm," I say to myself. "Glad I don't have that problem," as I run my hand over my half-bald head. "Then again, I wish I had some hair," I wistfully think.

As I daydream on the chair about a full head of hair, someone speaks to me in a broken English-Italian-Asian dialect.

"Massage, signore? Only 8 euros," she says.

Looking up I see this beautiful Asian woman, one of many who goes around to the sunbathers offering massage service, right there on the beach! "No, grazie," I say.

The Sicilian sun comforts me as the day wears on. After three hours on the beach and being sufficiently cooked (despite using SPF 60 sun block!), we decide to leave and get a bite to eat. After a quick shower at their facility (the shower is outdoors!), we dress and leave.

No day at the beach is complete without a quick pizza at an outdoor café, and that is exactly what we have. Gazing at the passers-by as we munch on our pizza (actually I am eating a pizza and Olga the goddess is eating her normal salad, hmm...must be something there!) I wonder what it would be like to live here all the time. Would I have to get one of those skimpy bathing suits to really fit in? No, I decided. Maybe my individuality might stick out a bit and maybe I look kinda funny in my American swim garb, but isn't that half the fun of being in a foreign land?

I return to Sicily on July 17th for the baptism of Massimo's son Marzio. In my bag is a new bathing suit: same style, different color!

5. Life by Drive-through Is Purely American

I have always said that someone can make a fortune if he or she opens up a car wash in Sicily.

When in Sicily a few months ago, Mt. Etna was once again spewing ash down on Catania. Waking up to find a fine layer of lava ash on the car, I decided to get the car washed. Unfamiliar with the location of a car wash, I questioned Massimo.

"Can you recommend a good car wash?"

"Alfred ," he replied, "the best car wash in all of Sicily is right in Catania."

After giving me directions to the "best" car wash in Sicily, I set off in search of this modern miracle. Sure enough, it was exactly like all the others I had seen in Sicily: three guys with a garden hose and a sponge slopping around soapy suds!

Cigarettes hanging from their lips, the guys talked a mile a minute as they lathered the car. When the conversation became animated, the hose was put down and arms flailed.

Tears rolled down my cheeks watching the Sicilian version of the Three Stooges. This was definitely the funniest moment I've experienced in Sicily!

After a good 90 minutes, they were finished...that's right, 90 minutes! The cost: 30 euros! (About $40).

When Massimo came to the U.S., a couple of weeks later, I decided to show him a real car wash. We rolled onto the rails of a local automated car wash. As we were being towed through the line, Massimo was in disbelief when the water first hit the car. He was like a child on a Disney ride! "Pazzesco!" he kept repeating over and over. When the giant cloth rollers lowered to wipe off the car, he ducked down on the seat sensing he was going to get soaked!

Drive through banks are another humorous experience. In Sicily, they don't exist! While here in the States, Massimo accompanied me to a drive through bank window. After filling the tube and pressing the "send" button, the tube zipped to the teller in the bank.

Confused, Massimo queried, "Alfred, what happened?" When given the details, he shook his head in disbelief.

"Alfred, such a thing could never happen in Sicily."

When I asked why, he explained. "Either the teller would deny ever receiving the money, or the person putting the money in would not give the correct amount! Only in America would you put your money in a little can and watch it go away!"

Again, tears rolled down my cheeks. Banking in Sicily is unique. Unlike here where we have huge banks with many branches, in Sicily, one local branch holds all your private information. Upon entering the bank you take a ticket, similar to that in a supermarket deli, and then you wait, and wait, then wait some more in line for service there. A banking "experience" often takes an hour in Sicily!

While Sicily isn't the most technologically advanced country in Europe, over the past five years it has made big strides. Nowadays ATM's are everywhere and the ATM's actually work on the weekends too! (This wasn't the case not too long ago).

Next month when I return to my beloved island, I will take my car again and get it washed, right before I go to the bank, of course!

Chapter Sixteen

A Very Young Mind

Last night my dear friends Lou and Cici came to dinner at my house. They brought with them a beautiful photo album of their recent trip to Tuscany and Sicily that we all enjoyed.

This was their first trip to Italy, and it was an unforgettable experience for them. Nearly four months after their return to America, their eyes still blazed with wonder as they recounted for us stories of their Sicilian trip.

Later on that evening, I pulled out my photo album of the trip nine years ago that I took with my daughter Jen and my mother, then eighty years old. (she is 88 years young today, and the reason I pulled out the album was that she is visiting us and I thought she might enjoy seeing those photos again)

Funny, when I pulled out that album, it was like we had been transported back in time.

I had set up that trip as an eightieth birthday gift for mom, and I brought Jen in order to give us a hand on the trip. At her age, I was fearful of the grueling plane ride. It was her first flight, after all.

My friend Saro Messina from Via Grande helped me set up the major surprise of the trip. He had tracked down the home of my mother's mother in Trescastagni, a home that she had left back in 1910, and Saro found out that the house, now owned by a retired judge named Messina, which had been completely restored. At the time, he graciously let us tour the house, and mom immediately recognized the bedroom of her mother, as it had been described to her in detail by countless stories when mom was a young girl.

I remember watching my mom sit on that ancient bed in that ancient bedroom. That image is still burned into my mind's eye and the look on my mom's face as she recalled her mother's spirit. It was simply unforgettable.

My daughter Jen later told me that she got goose bumps all over as she watched her grandmother go back in time.

Anyway, I had captured that moment with a photograph.

Last night, I opened that album and showed it again to Lou, Cici and my mom. My mother, even though 88 years old, recalled every second of that visit, nearly 9 years later.

Such is the effect of things emotional.

Every time I go to Trecastagni I stop the car in front of that house and reflect on that day.

I do not know what God has in store for my mom. She says that she is ornery enough to live until 100 (believe me, I agree). Here is what I do know: That day is burned forever in her mind and in Jen's too.

This is one of the countless vignettes that I have about Sicily: one of hundreds that I too relive everyday.

Sicily is in our blood, our souls. It is the essence of who we are. Every once in a while I get reminded of that!

Chapter Seventeen

At The Market and Shopping

1. The Market

Today I thought that I would take you shopping with me and show you how modern Sicilians shop. As you will see, it is now a blend of the old and the new.

Our first stop is in San Giovanni la Punta, a lovely village where my favorite hotel is located: the Villa Paradiso dell'Etna. I often go there for dinner, meetings, and the Sunday night over-35 disco: simply an elegant place. Back in the Second World War, the Nazi general Rommel was so taken by the villa's beauty that he had it converted to German military headquarters during the Nazi occupation. Today it is an elegant hotel.

As we drive by the hotel, we notice the palm-tree lined streets and the spectacular array of vegetation and flowers everywhere.

We are on our way to Le Zagare, a huge supermarket located in the Sicilian version of a mall.

This place is brand new—it opened four years ago—and local Sicilians still flock to the place.

As we drive into the parking lot, the first thing that we notice is, as usual, there are no parking spaces. This is a normal occurrence in Sicily. Sicilians build something, then build only 20% of the necessary parking spaces.

After squeezing between two very small cars (really, I understand now why people drive small cars in Sicily: they are easier to park. If I had my Toyota Forerunner with me, I am sure that I would still be driving around looking for a spot!). I head to the market.

First thing I have to do is get a cart. Here, all carts are chained together. To get a cart, you have to insert a 50 cent coin into the slot, which releases the cart. After shopping, when you return the cart, you get your coin back. Thus, carts aren't all over the place as they are in the states.

As we walk into the mall, we experience something unusual: air conditioning! This is a new occurrence. Prior to a few years ago, virtually no places except hotels had this amenity.

We walk into Le Zagare—it is huge and modern, very well lit, clean, and loaded with stuff.

On the first floor is the food: a terrific array of fresh fruits and vegetables. Today the harvest is in, so I will buy some figs. They are twice as big as those imitation things found in the States and cheaper, too. A kilo, about 2.2 pounds costs 3 euros, about $4.20. In the States, figs are about $1.00 each. Here I get 20 large figs for $4.20. In the States, this bag would cost 20 bucks. I pick up some fresh peaches too. $1.50 a kilo, about $2.25 for 2.2 pounds. In the States, peaches are $4.00 a pound, and they usually are terrible. Tomatoes, plums, lettuce, spinach, the story is the same, all succulent, all less than 50% of the price than the States.

My cart is half full with fruits and veggies. We need some cheese now.

Imagine a counter about 39 feet long. Imagine that this counter is shaped like a giant W—that is how many varieties of cheese there are today. Nothing wrapped in cello either. All fresh, all with no preservatives. I select *ricotta salata* (which is the only cheese that I use on my tomato based sauce), Asiago morbido (a soft white cheese that tastes yummy with fresh olives as an appetizer), and some local cheese for eating. Price is a little expensive right now, milk is high in Sicily.

I stop by the meat counter. Forget it! The meat is really poor in Sicily. A piece of meat the thickness of a pepper streak is their idea of a "steak". Boy, do I miss American beef! Same thing with the sausage, way too much gristle there for me.

I wistfully pass the meat counter and head to the fresh fish section.

Ah…..fish! All types, sizes, some of it still flapping around. Yikes! White fish is $20 bucks a pound! I stick to salmon (for some reason, Sicilians eat little fresh salmon and it is usually the cheapest), and calamari today, always cheap.

Next, I put the cart on a movable ramp and head up to the second floor. The ramp is magnetized and the cart doesn't roll backwards. Neat.

First, I head to the cleaning supplies section. I need something to put in with my wash because in Sicily the water is hard and calcium filled. I found it: Calco, a calcium neutralizer. Then I pick up paper plates. This is what we use during the week, no use washing dishes while we are here.

Then I check out the house wares section, the women's and men's clothing section, then the hardware section, the music section, on and on I go, looking at all three different things that they sell at a Sicilian supermarket and wondering why America doesn't have this type of one stop shopping (except tacky Wal Mart, that is).

Time to go.

At the check out counter another big difference: you must bag your own groceries. Plus if you want a bag, you pay 5 cents each! That is why Europeans bring their own cloth bags shopping!

I bag my stuff, return to my car, load it up, return my cart and get my coin back.

Now, I am off to the panificio for fresh bread.

2. Sicilian Banshee Women! Shopping

Oh my God! I witnessed first hand yesterday a 50% off sale at a discount store and lived to tell about it!

Here is the story:

Unlike America, stores can have sales only at certain times of the year. Usually, the price is the price until those times when stores are allowed a "Sconto," a sale which has to be advertised.

In Misterbianco, there are many big stores. Euphonics, for example, is like a Sicilian Best Buy; Auchon is the Italian equivalent of WalMart; StockHouse is the equivalent of a Filene's Basement or a Frugal Fannie. Anyway, the one store that I like to shop is Scarringi, almost like a giant Marshall's for men and women except they actually carry Big and Tall sizes, which I need.

Yesterday, the newspaper blared: "Sconti 50% da Scarringi". So I decided to go, just to observe things.

Oh my God! I saw Sicilian Banshee woman tearing, fighting, clawing, scratching, yelling, screaming: you name it, over this sale.

The place was packed beyond imagination. 10 cash registers were 25 deep. However, the sales were great. 100% wool sweaters, marked from $50 to $25. These sweaters would sell for $100 in America. Ladies jeans 10 euros, about $15.00. Everywhere I looked sales and screaming women galore.

After observing this circus for 20 minutes, I noticed that I was the only guy in this huge store.

I found out why.

All the men wait outside, smoking cigarettes, talking on their cell phones, generally waiting for their wives or girlfriends.

I went up to one guy and said that when I was in the store, I was the only guy in there.

He told me that I was lucky to come out alive. His wife actually trains for this day. Going to Scarringi every day for a week before the sale and putting things aside, so when the big day comes, she can quickly scoop them up.

Trouble is, another 500 or so women do the same thing, hence the hen pecking that I observed.

Yup! a "Sconto" after Christmas! Chalk that one off my list of things to do before I die. I was lucky to come out alive from there.

Chapter Eighteen

Seasons

1. Sicily in the Fall

Right about now in Sicily (October), roadside stands everywhere are selling the crops that have just been harvested.

Mushrooms of all varieties, an endless list of fruits and vegetables, chestnuts, olives and fresh *ricotta* cheese (Sicilians don't eat *ricotta* cheese during the hot summer months) are available right now as is, of course, wine.

Last year at this time I was gallivanting all over the Island and enjoying myself as I experienced Fall in Sicily.

The weather is still beautiful. Sicilians can usually go to the beach until mid-November and the average temperature is still in the high 70's every day.

The southwest portion of the Island is awesome: a great drive is the Palermo to Trapani to Sciacca route. With the seacoast hugging one side of your drive and gorgeous scenery on the other side, I bet that nowhere in Europe is as beautiful.

Over on the Southeast side of the Island, a drive from Siracusa to Pachino is a wonderful way to spend a day, and don't forget to sample some of the world's best tomatoes and melons when you hit Pachino. Since you are already there, drive over to Porto Palo, the ancient fishing village, and stop by Il Paladino for the best fish meal of your life.

I swear the prawns will melt in your mouth.

If you are up north, a drive from Messina to Cefalù will recharge the inner soul. Now, the sea is on your right and breathtaking mountains and valleys on your left. Don't forget to stop and take a picture of magical Enna on the way!

If you are in Catania, this is the time to take a drive to the Riviera Dei Ciclopi and enjoy the fishing towns of Acitrezza and Acicastello.

2. Fireworks! It Must Be Summertime in Sicily!

Trying to sleep in Sicily in the summertime is a tough proposition.

Just about every town and village has a festa on the weekends, and fireworks are a central part of the celebrations.

I am not talking about small fireworks displays, either. We are talking Fourth of July in Boston quality fireworks!

Sicilians are proud of their fireworks. One town, Bonnacorsi recently won the award for putting on Europe's finest display and this town has only 3500 residents!

If the noise from the fireworks wasn't bad enough, the time that they start is!

Last weekend the fireworks in Aci Sant'Antonio started at midnight and ended at 3:00A.M.!

Never have I seen a place people so crazy about fireworks! They can teach the Chinese a thing or two, I swear!

Next time I come to Sicily, the earplugs are the first thing I'm packing!

3: The Sicilian Morning: November

I love the crisp sunny November mornings in Sicily.

The sun is bright, but not hot. I can describe it as "light," very light in the morning.

Etna is covered with snow, and the view as I pass it by is breathtaking. A white-capped giant amongst the population.

First thing I did was to go food shopping. I go to a big market by the villa named Centro Squalo. I picked up fresh pears, oranges, bananas, some eggs and butter, some ham and cheese, milk, enough stuff to make lunches for a few days. Spent 46 euros on shopping.

The prices are going down here too as the Sicilian economy is also hurting.

Afterward, I stopped by Caffè Vittoria, a little coffee bar for an espresso and a brioche for breakfast. I sat outside and let the sun heal me.

I am still jet lagged and tired. I will be like this another day or two. However, breathing that Sicilian air while enjoying that espresso in the sun is just what the doctor ordered.

Tonight I am going to find "stocco," a regional fish soup that heals my soul.

I am connected to the world though. I have 2 cell phones (one American, one Italian), a home phone, and of course my Italian computer (all instructions are in Italian). So later on I will call into America and see what's going on. In the meantime, thank God I am in Sicily. I think I have said that a thousand times already!

Chapter Nineteen

Secret Recipes

1. Legendary Killer Peppers

Even though I pay the price all night long after eating peppers, those vitamin filled guys are wonderful. I can't live without them.

How can one possibly eat a sausage sandwich without one? Or a steak sandwich? Or even a cold meat sandwich? It's practically UnItalian/American if you do!

Can't be done.

Anyway, here is my late mom's all time authentic, right off the boat recipe for roasted peppers.

These little babies are legendary.

Sometimes, when I have made a particularly good batch, I feel like nailing one or two on the wall, just to admire them.

You should see the size of peppers in Sicily. Not like the puny ones here in the States.

Huge. Brilliant in color, succulent (gosh I love that word, never use it much though)

Anyway, you will need:

4 green or red peppers

¼ cup Extra Virgin Olive oil

garlic powder

Salt to taste

First, get a nice glass of wine as you gather all those things and sip it. This is the time to be thankful. Despite your harried life, a little mellow time first is in order.

Pre-heat the oven at 450 degrees while you think then over.

When you are nice and mellow, place the peppers on a cookie sheet. Cook those babies until they are BLACK all over. Turn then every once in a while.

Remove from the oven and put them in a paper bag. Let them sit there for a few minutes.

Take one out at a time and rub away the thin black skin. Tear the peppers after you remove the seeds and core.

Place the shards in a bowl and add the olive oil, and salt to taste. Mix well and add a squeeze of lemon.

They can be served hot or cold. They will last for a week in the fridge too. I love any sandwich that has these peppers on them. They make a wonderful sandwich with piping hot bread too. Yum.

2. Yummy Summer Salad!

My Mom's String Bean and Potato Summer Salad
Trying to find mayonnaise in Sicily is almost impossible. When you are lucky enough to find it, it is usually on one of the lower shelves, and the brand is unrecognizable.

Sicilians rarely eat mayo in the summer: way too hot.

However, this salad is found everywhere, is easy to make, and lasts a week in the fridge.

A great hot weather salad!

Ingredients:

3 or 5 pounds of a small potato, depending on how much you want to make.

1 pound of fresh green beans (fresh is great but frozen will do)
Olive oil
White wine vinegar
Salt and pepper

Directions:

If the potatoes have a thin skin, don't peel them. If they are course, peel them. In any case, boil the potatoes, drain the water and once at room temp, put them in the fridge to cool.

Do the same thing with the green beans: boil them for a few minutes, drain and chill.

After they have chilled for an hour or so, cut the potatoes in half if you used small ones or on quarters if they are big.

Combine the potatoes and the beans in a nice bowl. Add in olive oil (maybe about three or four tablespoons), the vinegar (same amount or to taste), salt and pepper.

Toss.

Then put back in the fridge for an hour or so.

If you barbeque, this is great with any meat or chicken dish.

In the wintertime, the same recipe can be used except skip the refrigeration steps and serve warm.

I love this stuff. Plus, it keeps for a good while in the fridge!

3. Feed Four For $15!

A Depression/Recession Meal that will feed for $15.00!
Forget red sauce this week. Try this one. One of my favorites.
You will need:
1 lb of a good quality linguine, spaghetti, or fettuccini
1 lb of medium sized shrimp either fresh or frozen
½ cup of a great 100% EVOO
Heaping handful of fresh parsley chopped
Pinch of hot chili flakes (not pepper!)
2 or 3 garlic cloves minced
Pinch of sea salt
In a large pot, bring your water to a boil adding a pinch of sea salt. Make sure the pot is big!
Cook your pasta according to the directions, stir frequently and taste it!
While the pasta is cooking, in a separate skillet heat the oil then add the garlic and hot flakes. Now add the shrimp amd toss for two minutes or until the shrimp are nice and pink.
Take one scoop of the pasta water and add into the mixture.
Drain pasta and add to skillet, now add your parsley.
Add more seasoning if you want, then serve!
That's it!
By the way, it is a deportable offense if you add cheese. No one adds cheese to fish dishes in Sicily!

4. The Perfect Pasta

The Perfect Dish of Pasta
There's nothing worse than over-cooked pasta. To me, that is a deportable offense.
Everyone has his/her own way of making that perfect dish, but really, mine is the best!
First, you must use a big pot. Not a small pot: a BIG pot. If a small pot is used, you will end up with a "Ball" of pasta all stuck together.
Bring the water to a full boil, not when the bubbles are tiny, when they are big.
Add a pinch of sea-salt. Fine is the best.
Read the cooking instructions on the back of your pasta wrapper.

If it says seven minutes, cook it for seven minutes.

I always taste the pasta at various stages of cooking, and I stir the pasta frequently.

Remove it from the stove when it is *al dente*.

Reserve one ladle of the boiling water right before you drain the pasta.

When you drain the pasta, do NOT rinse it. All the starch will go away, and you need the starch to help bind the pasta.

Immediately place the drained pasta in a skillet and now add in that ladle of pasta water PLUS your sauce.

Let it cook (no more than three or four minutes or when more of the ladled water evaporates) Stir occasionally.

Serve.

There you have it! The perfect pasta!

5. Alfred's Idiot-Proof Chicken Cutlets and Sauce.

This meal I think I have eaten my whole life. It was a staple in my house and tastes even better as left overs.

For the sauce:

Make a simple basil sauce:

1 or two bottles of *passata* (of course you can use your canned tomatoes, but I prefer passata)

2 or 3 garlic gloves minced

A good handful of fresh basil, chopped

Salt and pepper (to taste)

4 tbls EVOO

In a frying pan over medium heat, WARM the oil and the garlic. If the garlic turns brown, the heat is too high. After about 3 minutes, add in the *passata*, then salt and pepper.

Simmer for 20 minutes over a medium heat, then add in the fresh basil and simmer for another ten minutes.

That's it. Turn off the gas and start the cutlets.

For the cutlets:

1 or 2 pounds chicken breast cutlets with no skin. Breadcrumbs

2 cups fresh parsley, about one half of a handful

1 tbl. Parmesan cheese

2 eggs

Salt and pepper

A good frying oil (try a good vegetable oil)

Breadcrumb preparation:

In a mixing bowl mix thoroughly the bread crumbs, salt pepper, parmesan cheese and parsley. It's done. Set aside.

Chicken Preparation:

Wash the chicken in water and dab it dry. Take 2 eggs and beat them. Drag the cutlet first in the egg and then in the breadcrumbs. Gently pat the breadcrumbs into the cutlet. Be gentle here.

Cooking:

In a frying skillet, place the vegetable oil. Enough to coat the skillet, but don't drown the cutlets. Get it fairly hot. Place the cutlets in and fry on each side until golden brown. Remove and place on a plate and pat dry with a paper towel.

Final Product.

In an oven dish, layer the sauce and the cutlets. No more than two layers. Sauce, cutlet, sauce, cutlet, sauce.

If you want, add in a little more of the parmesan cheese on top.

Place in an over an 350 degrees for 10 minutes.

Serve.

Then go to heaven.

Many people serve a pasta (a long cut like spaghetti) on the side or serve the cutlets right on top.

Me? I like this in a nice sandwich with a good Italian bread.

Total Prep Time: 30 minutes once you get it down!

Easy!

Chapter Twenty

Americani-Siciliani

1. Lou and Ceci

My boyhood friend, Lou, and his wife Celia, worked side by side running their little market in New Hampshire day and night for over thirty years. During that time, their little market provided their family a modest living, sending one of their children on to higher education, and the other into service for our country. A little market being what it is, they worked seven days a week running their business and never took a single day off. Lou sometimes logged 70 hours a week of back-breaking work.

Lou is the son of a Sicilian immigrant. His dad, Sam, who died a decade ago, was a barber who immigrated to the States from the hillside town of Biancavilla, in Catania province. He worked, lived and died here, never returning to Sicily. Meanwhile, for Lou and his wife, days passed into months, and the months passed into years, and life being what it is, Lou's thoughts of visiting his dad's village, Biancavilla, became a far off dream. The closest Lou came was reading my emails about Sicily, attending the annual Feast of the Three Saints in Lawrence, MA and dreaming until a lucky break occurred. Completely by chance, he found a buyer for his business. After 30 years of blood and sweat, he decided to fulfill his dream. At age 55, never having stepped on a transatlantic plane, he decided to visit his dad's beloved Biancavilla and walk the streets of his father.

Knowing that I was taking a few people to Tuscany with me, Lou called asking for advice. I suggested that he and Celia first accompany us to Florence and Tuscany, in order for him to get a flavor of Italy, and then make arrangements to go on to Sicily and stay at my villa, and our Maria Pace would show him around. After thinking about it for a while, Lou decided to go for it.

Like two children eager to open Christmas presents, both husband and wife stepped onto Alitalia's cross-Atlantic plane wide-eyed. They took in every sight and sound Italy could offer first visiting Florence, home of Michangelo's *David*, and the wondrous Uffizi Museum. Lou wept when he saw the statue, and thanked me countless times for the Florentine experience. Traveling through the Tuscan heartland we stayed at my friend Paolo's agriturismo farmhouse.

Lou and Celia walked the hills, visited medieval towns, and reveled in the wonder of Tuscany, knowing all the while that the best was yet to come.

Last Saturday, I left him at the Florence airport: they were finally going to Sicily. For ten glorious days, Lou and Celia made up for three decades of toil and sacrifice. They visited Mt. Etna. They walked the streets of Taormina. They prayed at the church in Trecastagni. Lou experienced all the wonderful things that his father long ago told him about. He experienced a slice of life that existed only in his imagination.

Lou's voice recounting his profoundly emotional visit to Biancavilla rings in my ears. I treasure Lou's story. It is what invigorates me. To have helped someone in a very little way to experience what he had dreamed about makes all the toil and hard work on our part here at *All Things Sicilian* worthwhile.

After 20 glorious days of discovery Lou has returned to the States bubbling with stories. There is a spring to his step. He glows. One thing I know in my heart is this: I'll bet it is a lot sooner than three decades before Lou and Celia return to Sicily.

What do you think?

2. My Brother Tommy

In 10 days my brother, Tommy, and his wife Ellen will make a trip to Sicily and stay at the villa for a week. This time, he is bringing his four children. His entire family is very excited to make this trip. They will take part in the Feast of Sant'Alfio May 9-10th in our ancestral hometown of Trecastagni, the very same festival that our grandfather Gaetano helped start in Lawrence, MA over 80 years ago. While this is exciting for my brother all by itself, I think this trip will be especially poignant for Tommy, and I will tell you why.

Back in the year 2000, Tommy was as healthy as a horse. He always enjoyed a healthy lifestyle: golfing, playing basketball, jogging, playing the drums in his beloved blues band, in short, living an active life as he entered middle age. In the year 2000, he was 47 years old.

Then, a misfortune befell him.

Out of the blue one day, different parts of his body began to swell up and cause him excruciating pain. One day his hand, the next his foot, the next his shoulder, the next his knee. Almost every

113

day a different part of his body was blowing up like a beach ball. Startled by this turn of events to his health, he sought medical advice at one of Boston's best hospitals, and was diagnosed unfortunately with rheumatoid arthritis. This disease has no known cure; it only goes into remission. Bouts of pain when the disease is in its active condition are called "flare-ups". Instantly, Tommy's life changed.

My brother is also my best friend; we speak several times every day (there are only 2 years that separate us in age), and we have forever been the other's confidant. Thus, when Tommy took ill, it was like a knife had been pushed into my stomach.

Tommy's wife, Ellen, was (and is) an angel, offering support and encouragement to him and tried to make his life easier to manage. In May of 2000, I called her and suggested that she and Tommy join me for a trip to Sicily to attend the Feast of Sant'Alfio in Trecastagni. Tommy was very reluctant, fearful that one of those dreaded flare-ups would occur while in Sicily, ruining the time for him, his wife and me.

"Let's give it a chance, Tommy," Ellen suggested, and after a little prodding from both of us, he agreed to go.

In those days, I owned a villa in Pachino, too far from Trecastagni to travel every day, so we stayed at a great hotel in Naxos. The flight was uneventful and Tommy seemed to be relaxing by the minute as he acclimated to the climate and let the healing Sicilian sun embrace his body.

On May 9th, we paid a visit to the Church of Sant'Alfio. Tommy and I visited to light a candle for our parents and our grandparents. There are only two churches that I have ever been in where I have felt the presence of God. The first was in Assisi, at the Cathedral of Saint Francis, the second at the Church of Sant'Alfio.

When Tommy entered the church, a sudden calmness enveloped him. He separated from me and wandered about the church, gazing at the images of the Three Saints. I watched from afar as he wept. He said nothing. After fifteen minutes, we exited in silence.

For the last seven years, my brother and I have spoken little of this event. However, this is what I know: since that day seven years ago, his fighting spirit has returned, his flare-ups have been far less frequent, and he has returned to a healthy lifestyle of jogging and working out at the gym. He even hosts now a widely popular radio show called the "Sicilian Corner" along with his two buddies, Mike Lomazzo and Joe Tringali, on radio station WCCM (AM1490).

However, one event is burned into my memory. Shortly after he returned from Sicily, he was asked to ride on the "vara" at the Feast of Sant'Alfio in Lawrence, MA, an event that draws almost 100,000 people annually over Labor Day weekend. To be asked to ride the "vara" with the statues of the Three Saints is considered to be a great honor, and he was the first (and only) Zappalà ever to have been asked.

As he was on the "vara" that day, hoisting children and paying homage to the Three Saints, our eyes met and locked. Two brothers, from the streets of Lawrence, MA locked in a stare of thanks and wonderment that only we two were sharing that moment.

Now Tommy is returning to Sicily with his family. He and his family will return from Sicily with a renewed love of their ancestral homeland: the cycle is complete.

This year I will not go with my brother in May. My son, Matthew, and his wife, Lindsay, are expecting their first child, and I need to be here in the States for this blessed event. On May 9th, however, I will pause from my activities that day and think of my brother.

In my mind, again our eyes will meet and we will say nothing.

But we will both know.

3. Re-charging the Inner Soul

Bill Loconsolo is one tough guy.

This very successful Massachusetts building contractor is one of my dearest friends, and after years of cajoling, he finally relented and flew to Sicily two weeks ago to spend eight days with me sightseeing and dining.

"This place better be as good as you say, Al," he warned. "I've been all over the world and I know good food. The sights better be good, too" he added in his usual gruff voice.

"Just wait, Bill" I replied smiling knowingly. After his remarkably smooth flight with Alitalia I picked him up at the airport and headed north on the *autostrada* to my villa. The first sight that hit him was Etna, majestic Etna. For the first time in years, Bill's jaw dropped in astonishment.

"Nice little hill there, huh Bill?"

He said nothing. He was too busy enjoying all the sights and sounds of Sicily that were bombarding his senses and re-awakening long dormant emotions: memories of an immigrant grandfather who long ago held him on his lap and told him stories of his homeland. Bill's excitement was palpable. After letting him rest a bit and shower following his long travel, that night we selected Picolo Mondo in Via Grande for his first Sicilian dinner because I knew the owner, my friend, Carmelo, would prepare him a great meal. A wine aficionado, Bill picked up the wine menu and selected an expensive bottle of wine. "Bill, no need to do that here. Order the *vino rosso della casa*. It's outstanding and only 4 euros per liter." He wasn't disappointed.

As he savored Carmelo's succulent offerings, he kept repeating how the food tasted like the food that his grandmother prepared for him decades ago. Over an aperitif of *limoncello,* tears welled in his eyes as he related stories of his childhood with his grandfather. My big, tough friend had a sensitive and emotional side that was in full stage re-awakening.

Over the next few days, Bill sampled all the cuisine particularly enjoying the *cornetti con crema* and the *brioche con granita* alternating every day between the two for his breakfast.

For lunch, he loved the *arancini al sugo* (rice balls with sauce) or the pizza, and for dinner every night he sampled a different dish: *pasta alla Norma, pasta ai frutti di mari, calamari*...you name it, he ate it, with gusto. On *Ferragosto* after meeting up with our friend and colleague, Donnamarie, for a magnificent day at *La Romantica* beach we all continued to celebrate at Massimo and Anna's who invited us over their house for a traditional Sicilian family dinner. Bill truly enjoyed Anna's amazingly fresh, tasty and abundant courses.

Viewing the spectacular vista from the hilltop town of Taormina, relaxing in the splendor of the lido at Naxos and admiring, with the intense appreciation of a professional builder, the centuries old Sicilian architecture made Bill's days fly by. As each day passed, an increasingly more mellow and reflective Bill emerged. Eating a fresh fig bought from a roadside stand, he shared stories of his grandfather's fig tree in America. For every fruit and vegetable, every pasta and *dolce,* the scenes and memories from his childhood days came to life and I swear the stress lines faded away by the hour. Bill relished every minute of his trip.

The night before he left, my tough guy friend had completed his transformation.

"Al," he said, "Thank you. In 30 years I cannot remember such an emotional experience. I will never forget this week and I want to plan another trip with my family as soon as possible."

Yesterday Bill called me from the U.S.. He has already arranged a trip to Sicily over Christmas with his children and grandchildren and will be staying at the villa.

Chalk another one up to the charm of La Sicilia! And it couldn't have happened to a nicer guy!

Chapter Twenty-One

Sicilian Sunrise

This morning I made a point to get up at 6:00 AM to watch the sunrise from my deck. There is something about a Sicilian sunrise. The Ionian sea glimmers in the morning. It was dead calm on the water and there were perhaps a half dozen fishermen with those lamps on their heads trolling for squid and white fish. As I sipped my morning coffee and listened to Boz Skaggs play a little blues on my IPOD headset, and watching that shimmering horizon slowly come to life, I wondered how many times the scene I was watching has been repeated over the centuries. Listening to the seas very closely, I swore I heard the voices of the ancient Greek, Roman, Saracen and Spanish fishermen. Taking a quick shower, I checked my email and zipped to Viagrande for breakfast at the finest café in Sicily. The Grand Café Urna. I know the Giuffrida families, who have owned it for years, although the place has been around since the nineteenth century. During the Second World War, first the Germans and then the British took over the place as a field hospital. My friends Alfio and Michael, two "barristas" who have worked there for years, greeted me like a long lost brother. We gabbed for a while and I gulped my cappuccino and "cornetto con crema" with much glee. God, did I miss that place.

My next stop was to see my friend Alfio for fresh fruit and veggies. Listen to this: 1 kilo (2.2 pounds) of the freshest tomatoes you ever saw, freshly picked lettuce, onion, five oranges, strawberries from Etna, and giant green beans, with the giant pods: all for five euros! (about $6.20 USD).

Swinging by the Piazza San Mauro, I heard someone yell "Hey, Alfred!" Looking over my shoulder, it was my friends Peter Messina from the Italian Kitchen in Lawrence and Domenic Messina from Peabody Supply in Salem, MA. who were there for the Sunday's Feast of Sant'Alfio in Trecastagni.

Next thing I knew, Peter's mom who's 93 (!) years young, was cooking for us fresh pasta with basil sauce and "cutuletti,"chicken cutlets! Side dish was of *melanzana*, washed down with a fine red wine from a local winery. Mamma mia!

We chatted for a couple hours about Sicily. Both guys have a deep love for her and come frequently. In Peter's case, to visit his mom, who refuses to live in the states! Imagine that! A 94 year old woman, still spry as a chicken, who goes to church every single morning and hangs the wash of the roof—living alone. God truly blessed her.

Hanging on the deck last night and sipping Amaro Averna, that dark Sicilian "digestive" that everyone drinks here, Matthew's tune "So Much" and Roomful's "That Will Never Do" are absolutely ass-kicking tunes. Remember to bring your IPOD when you come! First thing I did this morning was to give one of the palm trees by my deck a haircut as it was blocking my view. I got a coat hanger and hung over the deck and reeled it in. My elderly neighbor, who caught me dancing on the deck last year in my underwear, thinks I am a nut. Old Mrs. Longo told me that isn't allowed. I told her in America it is a law that we do this once a year, so she shut up. Whew: That law degree comes in handy at times! The next thing I did was zip to the "supermarket" to pick up supplies including seven plants (cactus mainly, but also fresh basil) and planted them in my two flower trays. A bottle of Averna cost me 9 euro (in the States that same bottle is over $20.00), some cheese, eggs (orange yolks), olives, and of course, more fruit. The fridge is stocked pretty good now.

My "telecomando" works now. That is the gadget that opens the front gate. Last year, I had to keep climbing over it in the middle of the night as it was broken. Now, all I have to do is push a button as my car approaches and it opens. It actually opens. I am amazed. My Direct TV works. Five Russian stations (they have the best babes, I swear), two German, French, Spanish, CNN, plus a million other stations.

My friend Maria came to visit me. She asked if I had gained weight. I threw her off the deck. No really, it was nice seeing her and we caught up on things since the last time I was here. Tonight, Massimo is coming over, so we will have "things" to do. The weather is perfect. Warm, sunny, light breeze. No humidity. I decided to return in August too.

Chapter Twenty-Two

1. Ice Cream or Gelato?

I have been asked many times which I prefer, ice cream or *gelato*. The answer to that question is: it depends on where I am eating it.

Ice cream here is far better here than in Italy. On the other hand, gelato there is far better than here.

Why? Well, around here, there are many dairies that make their own milk as some of them are working farms. Their milk is creamy and fresh. In Italy, very few dairies re-direct their milk to ice cream producers as the vast majority of these producers make *gelato* as opposed to ice cream.

On the other hand, in Italy since only the large "commercial" manufacturers make ice cream, you will find that stuff in the frozen food aisle in the grocery store. It is just like ours: rock solid and not fresh.

Gelato in Italy, on the other hand is fresh, creamy, yummy.

Probably the biggest difference, however, is the prime ingredient: milk.

Here, most dairy cows eat wheat and grass chemically aided or genetically altered. This is not allowed in Europe. Did you know that 75% of all farmland in Italy would be considered "organic" here? The percentage is far less in the states.

That is why *gelato* tastes "different" here than in Italy. While some of it is tasty and very good and may even use imported flavorings from Italy, the basic ingredient, milk, is the difference-maker.

In the States there is nothing like licking a delicious ice cream on a hot day. The same holds true for *gelato* in Italy.

Price wise, *gelato* is much more expensive too. Why? Well, if you buy ice cream from "national" producers in the States, the ice cream is made in huge batches. In Italy, most gelaterias make small batches, sometime only a few liters at a time.

Here, toppings are usually candy, M&Ms, Reece's, chocolate, while in Italy fresh fruit or nuts is usually the preferred topping.

By the way, I have never found a banana split or a milk shake in Italy either.

Either way, ice cream or *gelato* is a great way to satisfy that sweet tooth.

Sherbet or *Sorbetto*? Here the differences are less. In the States there is a wider range of flavors while in Italy lemon is by far the most popular. Hmm! Writing this piece is making me hungry! Gotta go and find something sweet to eat!

2. Pupi Siciliani

If you browse around any market in Sicily, you will see Sicilian puppets for sale, and in researching the history of puppetry I was flabbergasted when I learned exactly how important they are to Sicily's history. Oral traditions merging history and customs, handed down from generation to generation, are what define Sicilian puppetry. Palermo has always been the epicenter of this tradition.

As a matter of fact, the Museo Internazionale delle Marionette (The International Puppet Museum) in Palermo, and the greatest museum of its kind in the world, has over 2,500 exhibits ranging from the most typical Sicilian *pupi* to other types of shiny armor marionettes from all over the world, including elaborate puppet-theater settings and apparatus. But why puppets?

The Teatro dell'Opera dei Pupi (Sicilian Puppet Theater) is world famous and virtually every city or town in Sicily had one, often operated by the same family who has handed down the craft from generation to generation.

Sicilian puppets are hand made, hand assembled and hand painted by three to four different people: a tin-maker who fashions all the metal parts, a wood maker who fashions all the wooden parts, a painter who paints the puppet and a clothier who dresses it. The "Puparo" is the one who assembles all the parts and is also the puppet master. Usually the figures depict the epic battle when the Normans drove out the Saracen (Arab) occupiers back in the 11th and 12th centuries. Charlemagne, Rinaldo, Angelica, the Saracen, and Orlando are figures that every Sicilian knows about, and each city takes pride in offering their interpretation to the story. One story that is frequently sung and represented by puppeteers accompanied by balladeers is *La Storia dei Paladini di Francia* by Giusto Lodico, which pits the forces of goodness versus the forces of darkness and usually ends in a fight to the death in the final scene. Other sources of stories come from Homer's *Iliad* and *The Bible* and the *Orlando Furioso* by Ludovico Ariosto.

Sicilian puppets are different from other European puppets because they are the only puppets supported both inside and outside by moving rods giving them the ability to move rapidly. As time progressed and the Arab occupation faded into history, puppetry became even more important as a vehicle of social and political commentary and the puppets, since they weren't "real" people, couldn't be prosecuted for what they said!

In my travels throughout Sicily, especially on the west coast, I have seen puppets that have staggered the imagination. Some have stood over three feet tall, with gold-plated armor costing over 3000 euros (over $4000!).

People from all over the world collect these important mementos of Sicilian culture and pass them down as heirlooms. We started to sell smaller versions of the puppets about 3 years ago on the internet and at our store (two sizes, small for about $20, large for about $60) and once a person buys one, they usually buy the other three sooner or later as keepsakes.

One Sicilian gentleman from the West Coast recently ordered 24 large puppets as centerpieces for his daughter's wedding, and told me on the telephone that his eyes misted up when he saw them on our web-site, as he never believed that they would be available in America.

As I travel Europe, I have noticed that all countries have their own version of puppets, and I wonder at how remarkable these little social commentators are and imagine just how much change they accomplished throughout European history. For those traveling to Sicily in the future; Trapani, Sciacca, Agrigento, Siracusa and Catania all have excellent puppet theaters for you to enjoy!

Chapter Twenty-Three

Most Unusual People

1. Renzino Barbera

A man of greatness died today. A man whose love of Sicily compelled him to push aside a busy and successful career in order to inform the world about Her majesty, was silenced today at the age of 90. Renzino Barbera, the father of my dear friend and brother Manfredi Barbera, passed this morning in Taormina.

Renzino was the Robert Frost of Sicily. A poet so eloquent in his expression that powerful men wept when they heard his words. Renzino was a living legend, and now he is gone on to a better place.

In my career, I have been in the presence of very powerful men many times. However, his presence was the presence of greatness.

A memory that was seared in my mind happened two years ago when I was in Taormina for a meeting with Manfredi. After the meeting, Manfredi invited Massimo and me to dinner with him and his wife, several other friends, and his father Renzino and his wife.

We met on the outside deck of the Excelsior Hotel in Taormina, the most elegant of them all. We shared pleasant conversation that evening. The sun was just setting behind Mt. Etna, which lay before us, creating a surreal and mythical setting.

The Excelsior is famous for its view of Etna. There is perhaps none better in Sicily, and the setting sun that evening created a picture in one's mind that could never be captured by camera or canvass.

As we enjoyed our aperitifs of Martini Bianco and a little cheese, olives, Manfredi's oil and a little bread, the frail old man rose from his seat to say something.

Renzino now didn't speak much anymore. His wife, ever at his side, had told us that he had not been well lately, and this night was special to him. He was sharing a dinner with his son Manfredi who lived in Palermo and didn't get over to Taormina all that much.

The table grew silent as he rose and looked at Etna.

After a moment of silence, he began to recite his famous poem on Etna. This poem was known all over Italy and is studied in all the schools. Each word that he spoke was electrifying, each phrase pierced the soul.

As the frail old man recited his poem, I realized that I was in the presence of greatness. It was a if Robert Frost in America was there, or T.S. Elliot, reciting their work. The poem was full of emotion and of love for his island, and especially Etna.

Even if you understood not a single word of Italian, you would understand every nuance of the poem and feel every emotion. It was a short poem, lasting only a minute or two.

When he finished, the lump in my throat grew and tears rolled down from my eyes. Looking over at his son, I saw that he too wept that evening. As a matter of fact, all at that table were weeping.

That moment is frozen in time in my mind's eye, and yesterday I relived it all day long.

Renzino had the gift of painting a picture with words, and that evening he bestowed his gift on that intimate little gathering of friends and family.

I last saw Renzino on New Year's Eve Day. I bumped into him and his wife while walking the Corso Umberto in Taormina. Kissing him on both cheeks and taking his hand, I asked if he remembered me and how he was feeling.

"Of course I remember you, Alfred" he said. "My body may be frail, but my mind is like that of an eighteen year old. Buon Anno (Happy New Year), Alfred"

I happened to have my camera with me that day for some reason. I asked his wife to snap a picture of us. She did. Last night I looked for that picture among the hundreds of pictures that I have taken over the years. After digging and sorting through many, I found it.

There he was, Renzino Barbera, with a dashing twinkle in his eyes and a shock of white hair, holding my hand in a gesture of friendship.

I remember kissing Renzino good bye. I am very happy that I did that.

Today, I think I will get that picture framed.

2. Joseph Privitera

This week I had an opportunity to meet via email a most unusual man.

He is an American of Sicilian origin and has had a most distinguished life.

While I am not normally overly impressed as I go thru life meeting people, this man gave me pause to reflect.

124

First of all, he has impeccable credentials. He not only is a college graduate, but holds a PhD, as well.

He is fluent in English, Spanish, Portuguese, French and Italian.

He was a college professor and had a distinguished career in the United States government.

He is a musician, playing many instruments: the flute, violin and guitar, to name three.

He has authored many books, on poetry, on the history of Sicily, on the language of Sicily, on the cultural influences that the Greeks, Romans, Saracens, Normans, Spanish, and Bourbons had on Sicily, and for enjoyment also a Sicilian cook book: 18 books in all.

Most of what has impressed me though is the way that he can paint a picture with words.

In our email exchanges that only recently have begun, I have been staggered by his eloquence of the written word.

Such that I look forward to his now daily notes.

He is a true Renaissance man..

A Renaissance man living now in the 21st century.

The fact that a Renaissance man exists in the 21st century is remarkable, given all the bad news that bombards us on a daily basis.

But do you want to know the most remarkable fact of all?

This gentleman, this Renaissance man, this linguist, this author, this musician, this historian, this cultural anthropologist is still very much active every day of the week creating, philosophizing, emailing, and living life to its fullest possible extent.

Did I tell you that he is 92 years old?

Yes, this week I met a most remarkable man.

3. Anna Privitera (Viagrande)

Gone are the days in Sicily when women wore black and cow-towed to their husband's whims. Today's Sicilian women represent a charge into the 21st Century and a movement for equal rights and female empowerment is ongoing. Although Italy ranks 72nd world-wide in gender-equality, it is gradually improving women's rights. The Sicilian woman is strong, intelligent, beautiful, and I want to introduce you to our 2009 *All Things Sicilian Woman of the Year*.

Her name is Anna Privitera and she was born and brought up in Viagrande, Sicily, a tiny town nestled on the slopes of Mt. Etna. She is the mother of two children, and a successful business consult-

125

ant in Catania. She has helped many Sicilian businesses bring their products to markets in America and the European Union. She identifies emerging companies, develops their business plans, and arranges for their investment money.

Shattering the "glass ceiling" has become the norm for women in America. In Sicily, however, women continue to struggle to make their way as business leaders. This hasn't stopped Anna Privitera. Juggling a schedule that starts daily by dropping her children at school and finishes in the evening keeping her home running smoothly, she traverses Sicily in relentless pursuit of helping the Sicilian businesses. Her clients are many, and vary from Sicilian travel companies to Sicilian olive oil producers.

Why does she do this? Her husband Massimo is a prominent lawyer and her family in general is filled with successful businessmen and professionals. She could have easily chosen to stay home and call it a day. The reason that Anna works so hard and selflessly sacrifices herself is three-fold. First, Sicily courses through her veins. She has an unrequited love for Sicily, which was ingrained in her by her father, Turi Privitera. He was a successful businessman who never forgot where he came from. In many respects, she carries on his philosophy today. Second, she is furiously fighting against the critical "brain drain" taking place in Sicily, where unemployment for college graduates is over 50%. In her pursuit to promote Sicily, jobs are created and critical intellectual mass stays in Sicily. Third, she is woman. She is 100% woman, a new breed, a leader in awakening the Sicilian woman and bringing her into the modern era, throwing off the yoke of oppression by the old school of thought.

For all of this, Anna Privitera is my hero. She is the embodiment of everything that is right in Sicily today, and that is why she is *All Things Sicilian's Woman of the Year*.

4. Leonardo Ciampa (Boston, MA.)

Bet you didn't know that we have our very own version of the Renaissance Man living right here in Boston, did you? Yup.

And we have chosen him *All Thing Sicilian's* "Man of The Year" Let me tell you a little about this treasure, this jewel. Someday, you will remember that I wrote these words. Leonardo is that talented, that gifted.

His name is Leonardo Ciampa and in my opinion he is a musical genius and a gem of a human being. I love Leonardo.

A lot.

Born in 1971, composer/organist/pianist LEONARDO CIAMPA is acknowledged as one of the most gifted and versatile musicians of his generation. He lives in Boston.

His compositions (which are considered "Neoromantic" in style include "The Annunciation Op. 23) (Cantata for chorus and strings); "Suite Siciliana Op. 14" (for violins, piano and orchestra), five organ recitals, a concerto for piano and organ, a piano quintet, and numerous sacred works. His works are published exclusively by CIC (Comprositorum.com)

Whew!

Leonardo has made seven European tours encompassing Italy, Germany and Austria and has also played in many International festivals.

He currently directs the Chapel Organ Series at MIT in Boston and I urge you to attend one of his concerts (he posts his schedule on his website www.leonardociampa.com)

For good measure, he has also written two books (*The Twilight of Belcanto* and *Don Lorenzo Perosi*) and has a popular blog (faultbook.blogsspot.com) and *Facebook* page too! Several years ago, the *Boston Globe* wrote "Genius is a word that pops up in conversations about Leonardo Ciampa" I love Leo. To me he is the essence of a pure soul. We have known each other for years and I treasure his friendship. Most importantly, Leo is of Sicilian origin and a true and genuine person. Bravo!

This month, Italian Cultural Heritage Month, we have picked Leonardo Ciampa as *All Things Sicilian's Man of the Year*. And no one deserves it more. Truly a remarkable person. Thank you for being Sicilian, Leonardo!

5. Mio Figlio Matthew

In life, a man can count on few things that bring him joy. My son Matt has always brought me joy. He is my son and my best friend, and I am fortunate indeed.

One of the most memorable experiences that I had in life was back in the year 2000 when Matt and I went on a father-son vacation to Sicily. A special bond grew that week between us: an unshakeable and unbreakable bond between father and son as we both explored our ancestral and cultural roots there.

That is not the only thing, however, that Matt discovered that week. You see, Matt is an extraordinarily handsome guy and he had, shall we say, a ball as he discovered the young ladies of Naxos and Taormina.

Many a night I recall him saying to me "See ya tomorrow morning, Dad" as he threw on some cologne and scooted off to who knows where for the evening.

All I know is that when we took off with the airplane a week later, both side of the runway were lined with beautiful gals crying and throwing rose pedals at the plane and shouting "Amore Mio, Matt!"

There is now even a disco in Naxos named "Chez Matt" in his honor.

Matt is now happily married to the most beautiful woman in America and she is now with child, which is due in June. "Little Al" I shall call him, and teach him too the ways of Sicily. Of course, "Little Al" will not be his name, only my special name for him. A nickname so to speak.

"One guy named Al Zappalà is enough, Dad" I was told a few hundred times by Matt. "We will restore the Zappalà name to prominence, don't worry, but first we got to get rid of the first name"

Matt now has a fine career as a government lawyer and is a wonderful father. I am bonkers over my granddaughter Noey, completely nuts over her.

In Holland the tradition is a little different. When a child has a birthday, people say "congratulations" to the parents as they were responsible for bringing him into this world. So today, I congratulate myself on the birthday of the finest son a dad could have.

In Sicily, we say "Auguri".

So "Auguri to the finest son in the world. I love you profoundly Matt!"

Chapter Twenty-Four

True American Diplomats

A Brief Introduction to This Story:

Sometimes, things happen that make you proud to be an American, very proud.

Let me tell you about the best that our wonderful nation has to offer and the heroes that I encountered yesterday here in Sicily. But first, I have to give you a little background.

Sicily is a land of the free today due in great part to the American blood that was spilled during the Second World War.

Thousands of American soldiers gave their lives late in the war as they fought alongside the British to free Sicily from the scourge of Nazi Germany.

Young Americans gave their lives in a foreign land fighting for democracy and today the bombed-out German pill boxes that remain in various parts of Sicily serve as a stark reminder of their courage, valor and sacrifice.

Since the war, a strong American presence remains.

Thousands of American servicemen and woman have been stationed over the years at our Naval Station in Sigonella, just south of Catania. A huge naval station and air strip is located there and our military now patrols the Mediterranean by air and sea from this strategically important base.

Many of our servicemen here have been deployed to defend American freedom from this base to Iraq, and more recently, to Afghanistan.

Yesterday, I had the good fortune to spend a wonderful day with some of these heroes, and to thank them personally for the sacrifices that they make for all of us, and the sacrifices also that their families make.

I do not think that I have ever been as proud to be an American after meeting these folks, who really are our finest and authentic true American diplomats.

Here Is My Story:

Robert and I looked at each other warily on Thursday night at Massimo's surprise party.

After all, he was a Met's fan from Brooklyn and I am a Red Sox fan from Boston.

"Just my luck," I thought to myself. "I have to spend the whole night with a Mets fan."

Only if he was a Yankee fan could it be worse.

For you baseball fans out there, the vision of Mookie Wilson's grounder going thru Billy Buckner's legs in the '86 World Series still haunts me and all of Red Sox Nation for that matter.

Now I have to spend a night in Sicily with this Mets fan.

Amazingly, by night's end, we had become firm and fast friends.

His name is Robert and he is the husband of Margherita, Massimo's best friend.

They had come to Massimo's party with their stunningly beautiful daughter Elli. Robert is very handsome, Margherita is very beautiful, so I could see where the daughter's beauty came from.

During that night, I learned a lot about Robert. He is of Puerto-Rican and German blood, born in Puerto Rico but reared in New York City. He spent twenty years serving our country in military bases all over the world and had met Margherita while stationed here. He now lives here running an extension school on the base while Margherita works as a physics teacher there.

They tried living in America for a few years while Margherita finished her advanced degree work in physics (she is a research paper away from a PhD in physics right now), but the call of Sicily proved too much for Margherita.

First she returned to get a job, and eight months ago so did Robert. He and I talked all night.

He told me many things. Mostly though, I saw a certain goodness in the man that only those willing to make the supreme sacrifice possess. In the military, he sacrificed himself for his country, and now he was sacrificing himself for his wife and family.

He is a stranger in a strange land, turning his back on a lucrative consulting job back in the States for his family.

As I drove home that night, I decided that I respected this man a lot.

Although I hardly knew him, I wondered if I could give up everything I had to go to a foreign country for love. A country that he was not connected to except thru Margherita. I thought about that sacrifice all night.

In theory it sounds romantic, but the reality of it is profound.

To my surprise and delight, on Saturday morning Marghetita called me.

"Alfred", she said. "We are having a barbecue at our beach house with some friends from the base. Would you like to come? Robert bought steak and ribs at the base and he will cook them for us."

American meat. Steak. Ribs. Here in Sicily.

Not that crummy Sicilian meat from cows that look like they have been run to death. American steak. From the grill. The aroma filled my nostrils in my mind. The words "Great!" couldn't come out of my mouth fast enough.

We met at a pre-arranged place in downtown Catania. The traffic was beyond unbelievable, but the aroma of a sizzling sirloin on the grill had changed my brain cells. I zigged and zagged. I had my yellow Fiat doing summersaults though the maze of Sicilian banshee drivers. I was an American about to eat a steak and I was not going to be denied.

"Watch out, buckaroos. Here I come!"

We drove about 25 minutes south of Catania, heading toward Siracusa.

Robert turned after a while down a dirt road and we entered "Villaggio Nettuno"…Village of Neptune, a gated community of beach houses. Robert's place was relatively Spartan but secluded, surrounded by trees, and lovely. The beach was located about 150 meters away, just on the other side of the trees.

Also arriving at the same time were the guests that Margherita had invited. Two very special families from the base.

One family hailed from Rochester, NY and Virginia. Paul and Maria, and three wonderful children Lessia, Sofia, and Michael. All the children were blond haired, blue eyes, dolls. Maria worked on the base as an elementary school teacher, and Paul was just about completing his second three year tour in Sicily. The children has spent almost all their lives in Sicily I later found out.

Maria told me that she and the kids would probably return to the States sometimes this summer.

"What about Paul? " I asked.

"He's being deployed at Christmas to Afghanistan."

That news hit me in the gut.

It was said stoically by Maria. It was said by a military wife, just as willing and eager to make a sacrifice for our nation as her husband. She would mind the three kids in America, aged two, five, and seven, while her husband served his country. No regrets, no sadness. A steely willingness only to do what was necessary for their country.

We went to the beach while Robert prepared the grill.

The day was sunny; the sand was rock free, the water warm. I dove into the Mediterranean and felt the saltiness on my body, a different kind of feeling than back in America. This was the ancient Mediterranean and I was swimming in a spot that the ancient Greeks and Romans swam two thousand years ago. Spiritually, I felt cleansed.

Soon after, another family from the base joined us. Chris and his wife Gretchen, and their two little daughters Bri and Eva.

Chris also was a vet, and now he and his family lived in Sicily while he worked running construction projects on base. Beside Sicily, he has served in Guam.

They were from the Pacific Northwest, the state of Washington. I could tell immediately that Gretchen was supremely well suited for motherhood and Chris was indeed very fortunate to have found such a woman.

Her life was devoted to Chris and the family. Her vocation was that of a mother, and she was home schooling the children.

Suddenly though, the aroma of a sizzling sirloin hit my nostrils.

All this time, Robert was working the grill, and those babies were ready.

Man, were they ready. That first bite of steak was, well…heavenly.

Perfectly grilled, prime USDA beef, cooked by a great guy in a wonderful setting, surrounded by authentic American heroes.

I was overwhelmed, actually.

I ate two steaks.

Yup! Two whole steaks. No bread though. Just good old American protein.

Driving home after such a wonderful and moving day, I mulled over the lessons of life that I learned today. Lessons that I will not forget for a long time.

I was fortunate to catch a glimpse of sacrifices that people make for all of us, gladly and willingly, and for our nation.

I was humbled to be an American. These people, every one of them, are my heroes, and I thank them for service to our nation.

Before I left, I pulled Paul aside. I told him that I was proud of him and I will pray to God to protect him while in Afghanistan.

For a moment there, his steely blue eyes softened. He said "thank you".

I actually got a little knot in my throat, truth be told.

As for Robert?

Well, I had to do something symbolic as a way of saying thank you too.

I had to give him a symbol of our new found friendship: something unique, something that he would remember.

I had such a gift and I gave it to him.

A Boston Red Sox hat that I brought with me.

I gave a Red Sox hat to a Mets fan.

God, Billy Buckner would be so proud.

Chapter Twenty-Five

Driving: Introduction, Prelude and Aftermath

Introduction

Driving in Sicily and Italy is fun, if you are a NASCAR driver, that is.

I am not kidding when I say that my heart is in my mouth every time I get behind the wheel in Sicily.

First the obvious: forget driving in the big cities. Only those with a death wish should drive in Rome, Florence, or Milan. Only the stoutest of heart can survive these cities. If you are like me, then MAYBE you can manage the back roads of Italy and Sicily. I said maybe because road signs always disappear at key times when you drive, and north means east and east means south it seems.

Renting a car is fun too. First, the size. A "sub-compact" in Europe translates into a sardine can here in the U.S. I am talking teeny-weeny. If you stand over five feet four inches tall and weigh over one hundred and fifty pounds, this class of car is not for you, definitely!

A "compact" car in Italy is really a "sub-compact" here in the States. Not teeny-weeny, just tiny, tiny: a slight improvement. While I can fit into one of that size, I had to get used to driving with the steering wheel in my chest, my face against the windshield, and my legs against my shoulders. Getting into one of those miniatures took me half an hour once!

"Mid-Sized" is acceptable, barely acceptable. Ford Focus or Fiat Punto-size means that if you travel with four pieces of luggage, only two fit in the "trunk" and the other two go in the back seat, standing up!

Yup! European rental cars are real pieces of work!

Gas? Sure, by the liter! A gallon of gas nowadays is nearly $7.00. THAT is why people drive these tiny little things! The gas station attendant puts the gas in by the eye-dropper, I swear!

The horn? Probably more important than either the gas pedal or the brake, I have read that Italians honk their horns more than any other people in the world, really!

Thus, you have to be a daredevil if you want to drive there! Maybe I am exaggerating a bit, but driving around Italy certainly is an adventure, for sure. It is not unusual that when driving on a beautiful road in the backwoods of Sicily, you must pull over so that a herd of goats or sheep can cross the road or you find yourself behind a guy in a horse-drawn cart, cars zooming by in the other direction so you can't pass him! I love that one!

Better still, ever see a tiny truck with THREE wheels (one in the front, two in the back) loaded two stories high with bales of hay and the whole thing leaning to the right driving on a highway? Do you try to pass or what?

I think you are getting the picture.

In Catania, I particularly love to park my nine foot long car in an assigned parking space that is nine feet one inch long. By the time I have backed up, pulled forward, backed up and pulled forward seven or eight hundred times, I am ready for the shower!

Small cars, high gas prices, non-existent parking spaces are nothing compared to driving in a mountain top town like Taormina, Bruccheri, Bronte, or even parts of Palermo. Some of the streets in these towns look like the downward slopes of the Coney Island rollercoaster! The roads virtually a vertical drop! Try BACKING into a parking spot on one of those slopes! Believe me when I say that I have burned out one or ten clutches and countless emergency brakes!

Anyway, isn't part of the allure of travel the adventure, you say? Sure it is, if your name is Evil Knievel, that is!

Prelude

The helmet is ready and so am I.

I stayed up all night reviewing Sicilian cuss words and gestures. Today is the test.

In a few moments, I will be leaving the secure confines of my condo and heading out into the great unknown: downtown Catania during the morning rush hour.

Catania during the morning rush hour is Manhattan gone mad.

A city full of crazed and possessed drivers intent on squeezing, cutting off, tailgating, blowing the horn, gesturing, flailing, and generally going completely nuts, all at the same time.

I am prepared. I am strong. I am a veteran of the Boston commute. However, I fear my preparation inadequate. I am a boy among men, crazy, possessed men.

Massimo called me last night and asked if I could pick him up at 9:00 AM at the Toyota dealership in Catania, and I stupidly agreed to do so.

He has a Toyota Rav and it must be serviced. His wife is unavailable, plus he has to be in court by 10 o'clock. I am his only option.

Yikes.

First I have to find the dealership. He gave me great directions. "Alfred, just go straight!" he said.

Straight to where? Straight to hell? Straight to Valhalla? Where? Doesn't he realize that Catania defines the word "maze"? Doesn't he realize that anyone who ever flunked traffic management in all of Europe works for the City of Catania? Doesn't he know that a red light means go faster and a yellow light means step on it? Doesn't he realize that there isn't a single straight road in the whole city?

Hasn't he seen all the roundabouts there? Where banshee drivers enter at 60 miles per hour and are oblivious to even the most rudimentary rules of the road?

Plus the motor bikes that drop from the sky like manna, attacking from all directions. north, south, east, west, and up and down too.

Yup. Today is the test. The supreme test of skill, guts, determination, guile, and survival.

Just so the guy can get his oil changed.

Geez.

Anyway, I have done my exercises, I am loosened up, I have broken a sweat. My years as an athlete at Austin Prep and Boston College will now pay dividends. My lighting quick reflexes are ready.

I will become one with the road. I will rule it. I will zig and zag. I will squeeze and pound the metal. I will swerve and sway with my car. It will become an extension of me.

I am ready. Completely and utterly ready for war. Hit me with your best shot: fire away.

If I survive, I have promised to the gods to make a sacrifice of three chickens and one sheep. I will burn incense all day for three days and ring little bells every hour. I will wear a hair vest.

Catania during rush hour.

Like driving the Cannonball Express with no brakes and no steering wheel.

But I am man. I will survive.

I am a finely made American machine.

All I gotta do is keep saying that to myself, I think.

B: Aftermath

Ha.

We showed 'em. Did they really think that Al would be intimated?

I am pleased to report that yesterday's excursion to Catania during rush hour to find Massimo at his car dealership was a success.

My finely honed reflexes carried the day, and I zigged when I had to zig and zagged when I had to zag. The old pedal was pressed to the medal, believe you me.

My little yellow Fiat responded like a champion horse at the Kentucky Derby.

Call me Mario now, as in Andretti. Al Andretti I will now answer to.

The only set back is this morning my neck is a tad sore.

I had never seen such a concentration of spectacularly beautiful women in one place before and believe me, THAT was the sole impediment yesterday.

I couldn't keep my eyes on the road.

Mamma mia!

Here and there I looked. My neck felt like one of those little bobber things that people place in the back of their cars by the time I arrived home.

Thank God I am an old man.

Masssimo laughed like hell as he pointed out one after another.

"Alfred, do you see this in Boston?" he asked.

Now don't get me wrong. American women are indeed beautiful. However, the beauty here is well, different.

"Massimo," I said "I am just goofing around. My grandfather Gaetano always told me that when I stop looking, then that is the time to start worrying," I said.

Anyway, a little Ben Gay did the trick and today I head into Acireale for a super secret meeting that we are having with some big shots there.

The deal is almost complete, and once I have it fine tuned, I will make the appropriate announcements.

When I do, you will love it, believe me.

Chapter Twenty-Six

Places

1. Road Trip!

Today was one of those days where I put a lot of miles on the tiny Ford Focus that I am driving.

First thing, this morning Massimo and I went to the gas company in Acicatena. Since I signed the lease yesterday, the gas, water and electricity have to be switched. Here, you have to sign 5 different documents and pay 14 euros for the privilege of getting robbed every month!

After that experience, Massimo went to Catania and I took a leisurely drive to Giardini-Naxos, where I had to pick up some brochures for our trip in May to the Grand Beach Hotel.

The hotel is undergoing renovations right now, but Blanche in the office gave me a handful of flyers. We are planning on taking a group of 30 to Sicily from May 7 to May 16.

I love Naxos. The view looking up from the bay to Taormina is one of the prettiest in all Sicily. Naxos was where I met a former love, and for me when I pull into that town, there are bittersweet memories. What's that old saying? It's better to have loved and lost than never to have loved at all. Anyway, after a quick cup of espresso at my friend Roberto's place, I headed to Taormina: the Pearl of Europe.

I took the shore road to Taormina, a spectacular shore drive that winds around Naxos Bay and boasts the most magnificent panoramic ocean view you could possibly imagine.

Half way up the mountain, I stopped the car and took some photos. I don't know exactly why I do this since I probably have 100 photos of the same view. It seems like I am compelled to take them, I guess.

Today the sun was shining brilliantly and the glistening water made for yet another great shot.

Preceding up the cork-screw road that leads to Taormina, I found myself constantly turning the wheel first hard right, then hard left, then hard right. Well, you get the picture.

Years ago, I found a free spot to park the car and every time I hit town, it is waiting for me. Today, it was no different. A free space!

I love being alone in Taormina. I love to watch the faces of the tourists. Today there was a group from China gawking at things. Another from Germany. As I walked up Corso Umberto, I bumped into a group of old timers from Florida who were traveling as a group. By old timers, I mean OLD timers. I was amazed at this particular group. It was like the local nursing home made a field trip, I swear. A sea of blue haired woman and a singular elderly guy. I betcha he was having a lot of fun with those gals, though.

One of the old ladies told me that Alitalia had lost almost everyone's bags last week when they arrived in Palermo. She told me that she had been wearing the same undies all week.

Somehow, that visual stuck with me, and I kinda lost my appetite there for a while.

After walking around some more and stopping at my old hang out the Wunderbar for another espresso, my appetite came back (by then I had blocked that visual of old lady bloomers hanging out the window to dry out of my mind), I grabbed a pizza at a nearby pizzeria.

There, I met another American couple (normal age) and we talked about politics and travel. Great couple.

On the way home, as I zipped on the autostrada, I noticed Etna for the 100th time. She is covered with snow and again I pulled over to take yet another shot of her majesty.

BTW: All the shop owners were complaining about a lack of business/tourists, and for the first time ever, I saw some of the top end shops with big 50% off signs on the windows.

Oh yeah, gas here is 1.25 euro a LITER. That is 5.00 euros a gallon, or about $7.50 USD a gallon.

And they tell me the prices are way down too.

Tonight, dinner at my pal Salvo's restaurant, The Heritage!

2. Paradise on Earth: Nicolosi!

Let me tell you about my paradise on earth, a little mountain village named Nicolosi that I often travel to when I want to think about all the good fortune that I have been given in life.

Nicolosi lies nestled in the hills of Etna, about 14 km. from the crater.

In 1998, when I was here, Etna had a fierce eruption and lava threatened the town. Actually the tourist area to view Etna was destroyed. It is called Rifugio Sapienza and everyone thought Nicolosi would be buried.

Legend has it that the local priest took a crucifix and placed it on the road in front of the lava flow and that it miraculously stopped.

I cannot confirm the story, but people here live in a sort of peaceful co-existence with the mountain, They say that Etna gives and Etna takes away.

Etna gives by leaving fertile soil that can grow anything. Right now, peaches are being harvested, the kind that when you bite into them the juice squirt everywhere and taste delicious.

Plums, mulberries, melons, apricots are being harvested now and vendors line the road up to Nicolosi selling their harvest at less than half the price that you can find in America!

Etna takes when her fury is awakened, destroying everything in her path. Thus a balance between life and death exists here, both in reality but also in the way the locals view life.

The solitude of Nicolosi is breathtaking to behold. Stands of trees line the mountain as far as the eye can see. Beautiful trees. The air is cool, crisp. You would never know that it was 90 degrees just a few miles away.

The town is post card pretty, clean and well cared for: a joy to behold. Tidy Bavarian styled houses are nestled everywhere.

I stopped at an outdoor restaurant for a cup of espresso and ended staying there for 2 hours enjoying the ambiance of the moment and thanking God that he once again allowed me to travel to this wondrous place.

Nicolosi is noted for its spas and mountain hotels. It is small. Less than 8,000 live here, but it is a prism of life.

I love Nicolosi. I think next Sunday I will go there again and think about my good fortune and hope that someday you too can experience with me this wondrous place.

Tomorrow I travel to Trescastagni, my ancestral hometown and will tell you the story.

3. Trecastagni: A Healing day

This afternoon I took a drive to my ancestral village of Trecastagni, about half way up Mt. Etna.

The day was cloudy, and the mountain was hidden by dense clouds. Rain clouds.

As I went up the mountain, a trip I have taken a thousand times, I finally felt at home. The tension and fast pace of America has taken me three days to shed.

On the side of the road, peddlers are selling grapes, persimmons, cactus pears (*fichidindia*), and artichokes. The same guys wearing the same clothes from the last time I was here, I swear. You know the picture: scruffy-faced men with those Italian caps, beat up worsted suits, a cigarette dangling out of their mouths.

I stop the car and for 3 euros I pick up a kilo of grapes and 4 persimmons. Yummy. Tonight, I will eat them.

After a fifteen minute drive on the winding and narrow strada, after passing new construction here and there, I arrive in Trecastagni.

I am here for a reason today. One of my dear friends from Massachusetts, a devotee of Sant Alfio, is having a hard time with a business investment. He is on the verge of losing everything. Last week, he stopped by the store and we talked. I told him that I would say a prayer fro him and his family. Plus, I always stop by to the church of Sant Alfio to say a prayer fro my 2 grandfathers, who were raised there, plus my dad. I have this prayer routine, as we all do. Basically I start from the top and name just about every one I know, and ask Sant Alfio to intercede on their behalf.

Not that I am a religious fanatic, far from it. I have sinned so much in my life (I am a lawyer after all), that not only is he going to have to go to bat for me when I hit those pearly gates, but just about the entire congregation of saints will have to as well.

I got to the Church as 3PM…and it was closed. I asked a worker (they are re-doing the facade and 4 workers were on staging working like bees) at what time the church opened. He told me at 4PM.

I had an hour to kill, so I headed to the town square for a espresso and to see the old timers there.

They gather at the square all day long and solve the world's problems, as countless Sicilians have done in countless village squares for a millennium.

Taking my spot on a bench, I enjoy the ambiance. The air is fresh, clean. Mountain air. On that bench, I think of Alfio, my grandfather. He used to come at this very place as a teenager before immigrating to the USA. I think of him, wondering if he every sat on the bench that I was sitting on.

The palm trees were calm. The roses in the square a vibrant red, pink. The water monument in the square's center shut off for the winter ahead.

Fall in Trecastagni.

This moment was worth 9 months of hard work back home.

At 4PM I returned to the Church, and said my prayers. I feel good in that place...a certain healing takes place, I think.

After a 30 minute visit, I leave.. I head to Viagrande to the tobacco shop, and pick up a cannoli for a treat later tonight.

Back on that mountain road I think to myself: "This is why I come here."

4. Hey, Where's the Pepto-Bismol???? Castelbuono.

Ever hear of a tiny Sicilian village named Castelbuono? Neither did I until the night that Manfredi decided to invite Olga, Massimo and myself to dinner there in late January. We were in Palermo on business and a dinner invitation (especially when someone else is picking up the tab) is very nice after a tough day's work. Our business with Manfredi had concluded and we first retired to the hotel to rest a bit and freshen up. Manfredi told us that he would pick us up at 9:00 PM. Although that is a little later than I normally like to eat, Sicilians usually eat at that hour. I hoped that the meal would be quick so we could return to our hotel. Little did I know what was in store for us that evening.

After picking us up, Manfredi first headed to the port area for an "appetizer" (You can read about that adventure in our March edition of All Thing's Sicilian's Newsletter). After downing a bottle of Pepto-Bismol, we headed to the *autostrada*. Oddly, once on the highway we found ourselves traveling east, AWAY from Palermo. Massimo inquired where we were headed. "Castelbuono," Manfredi replied. I asked Massimo where Castelbuono was, and as usual, Massimo hadn't a clue. "Someplace, Alfred," can you image THAT answer?

Knowing that we were headed for an adventure, we settled in for a long car ride. An hour later we zoomed past Cefalù. By zooming I mean exactly that. Manfredi is one of those banshee Sicilian drivers: 120 kilometers per hour. We continued zooming east. Finally, at 11:30 PM, we exited the *autostrada* at Castelbuono.

"My god, it's nearly midnight and we aren't even there yet!" I whispered to Olga.

Well, another hour AFTER exiting the highway, having driven up the side of a mountain in a cork-screw manner, circling round and round and round forever, it seemed, the town of Castelbuono appeared. At nearly 1AM we arrived for dinner!

Anyway, we met up with some of Manfredi's pals who had kept the only restaurant in town opened until we arrived and we ate and ate and ate: mushrooms in every form, shape, variety, taste, and recipe you can imagine. I later found out that Castelbuono was THE mushroom place in Sicily and that is what the mountain produces mushrooms.

Except, of course, Massimo can't eat them! Allergies. There wasn't a single item on the menu without mushrooms in it. Zero. The poor guy ended up eating spaghetti with olive oil and garlic and he hates garlic (if you can imagine an Italian who hates garlic!).

Olga on the other hand was in heaven. She loves mushrooms. No, she adores them and relished each shape presented to her with gusto and appropriate appreciation. Me? I enjoy mushrooms, but for heaven's sake after 7 different courses, I had my fill. Yet on they came. The March of the Dancing Mushrooms. At 4:00 AM we headed home. Manfredi was content, so was Olga. Massimo was hungry, and I was now nursing a bad case of indigestion.

"Alfred," Manfredi queried. "Tomorrow night I have another surprise for you. Do you like fresh calamari?"

5. Cefalù: Another Hidden Jewel!

Last summer I wanted to go to Cefalù but for some reason was never able to make the trip. This time, a visit there was at the top of my list. After visiting this little jewel, I decided that I will make it a point to visit there again next summer and to really get to know the place.

Here's my story about our adventure:

I started our from my villa in Aci San Filippo one bright Sunday morning two weeks ago and headed south on the *autostrada* past Catania, then followed the indications toward Palermo.

Traveling through this stretch of highway has always been a favorite of mine. The Plains of Catania offer a completely different view of Sicily, traveling first across lush farmlands of wheat and vegetables and then slowly watch as the terrain turns barren as I progressed inland into a wondrous starkness, and then watch again as the mountains appear magically offering again a completely differ-ent texture of the Island.

While driving on the Plains (the drive through this stretch take about 90 minutes), I caught nine different variations of the color green and six different variations of the color brown. I bet this has inspired an artist or two or fifty over the years.

When the road to Palermo split into the East-West direction, I followed the indications east toward Messina. About 20 miles down the highway was the exit for Cefalù.

This charming and graceful little town faces the Tyrrhenian Sea from a promontory overhung by a huge, rough outcrop of mountains.

Because of its favorable climate and outstanding natural and artistic features, I realized in two seconds why Cefalù was consid-ered to be one of the best tourist jewels in Sicily.

It carries a terrific tourist trade and as I wound my way thru the quaint cobblestone streets toward the Cathedral, I was reminded of Taormina, or on the mainland of Assisi.

The town hugs a white sand beach and I imagined that in the summer the place must be jammed.

The major reason I came to Cefalù was to see the Cathedral built way back in the first half of the 12th century by Roger II and I was absolutely blown away.

The monumental interior has the characteristics of a basilica; the nave is divided from the aisles by powerful columns with artistic Roman and Corinthian flourishes. The arches have Arab influence.

The outside facade is framed between two powerful towers light-ened by rows of lancet windows, Moorish style.

In short, I was absolutely floored by what I saw and in my case anyway, I think that this Cathedral is one of Sicily's best.

After a wonderful walk on the boardwalk and checking out what the Moroccan vendors were selling in their little sidewalk tables, I headed home content in the knowledge that I really had found something special.

Mark the name Cefalù down. If you get to Sicily, make sure you hit this spot. Maybe I will see you there myself!

6. Mt. Etna....Aglow For the Holidays

Mt. Etna, Europe's youngest (only 65,000 years old!) and most active volcano, has been very spirited lately. Since last September, she continues to remind all of her presence. I have witnessed her eruptions four times over the years, leaving in my mind an unforgettable impression of her might and her beauty. The mountain is compelling.

The ancient Greeks and Romans viewed the mountain with awe, fear and respect. The mountain was the home of Vulcan, God of Fire and Cyclops. Ancient mariners used her light as a beacon as they traveled the Mediterranean Sea and more than once her might has destroyed those who love her most.

Modern Catania, for example, has been completely destroyed twice over the centuries by Mt. Etna. Excavations currently underway in Catania show an ancient city 21 feet beneath the present one. However, she loves as well. Her fertile soil has fed millions over the centuries and has inspired all that are in her presence.

Surprisingly, the name Etna has been used since ancient times but the meaning has long since been lost. The Arabs were so struck by her during their occupation of the Island that they called it "Mongibello" the mount of mounts, the mountain that defines all others. If you visit the Island, be sure to take an excursion to Mt. Etna. Even if the mountain is erupting, excursions still take place, as the volcano "blows its top" only in certain areas and directions. For those of you who hike, the Park of Mt. Etna has wonderful hiking trails. The skiing is terrific there during the month of March. Mount Etna Round Trip Railway offers a three and a half hour excursion around the mountain (a safe distance too), that stops at Misterbianco, Belpasso, Paternò, Biancavilla, Adrano, Bronte, Randazzo, Giarre, Riposto plus 10 other villages. I am sure those of you whose parents, grandparents, aunts or uncles came from these villages are smiling now.

7. Naxos

My friend of many years by the name of Roberto owns this great outdoor restaurant and watering hole named Caffé Sikelia in Giardini Naxos across the street from the Hilton Hotel. He and his beautiful sister Sonya run the place. He is incredibly handsome ,suave, multi lingual, intelligent and she is his female counterpart. For years I have made this place my base of operations for social "gatherings" and business meetings. As a matter of fact, over the years I can recall many fond gatherings, although now I cannot recall

145

any of their names. This guy is my idol. He owns half of Naxos it seems, several restaurants, many shops, real estate, other businesses, but he is happiest greeting people at Sikelia, his first love. The café was recently re-decorated this winter with new café tables, terrific lighting, a great sound system that doesn't give you a headache, a terrific line up of mixed drinks, and killer pizza, pasta, and deserts, all home made. If Roberto's place were in the North End in Boston, the line would be blocks long. Anyway, here is where I hang out, and God willing, here is where I will always hang out.

One of my fondest memories ever was back about ten years ago when I took my son Matthew to Naxos for a father-son vacation that was one week of pure unadulterated fun. Matt hit every disco in town that year and did his best to extend an official greeting to every female who entered town limits. He succeeded every night, I think, and to this day every time I mention Naxos, a kind of euphoric glaze comes over his face and I think I see him levitate a little. Now that he is happily married with two kids, this place, I am sure, is in his Hall of Fame.

Anyway, Roberto last night told me that some lucky gal from Acireale finally snagged him and he is engaged to be married. At age 45, he appears to be "off the market," although when I asked him when the happy day is, he told me that he wanted to enjoy being engaged for a while before making plans. This may be a year or two or five! In any case, Roberto is my dear friend and we have shared many experiences together. I usually go there once a week (I have to recover the other six days as I am approaching the age where I am running out of runway and the old grey mare ain't what he used to be) and I will bop down there again next Tuesday. When I return in August, when the "tourists" from Holland, Germany, Russia, and England are there, then I again will show them the meaning of "American-Sicilian" hospitality.

8. Capo San Vito

Capo San Vito.
Ever hear of it?
Neither did I until Manfredi Barbera, our olive oil producer, told us that is where he was putting us up after our meeting in Palermo last week.

"Alfred", he said "It is a beautiful beach resort. Bring your bathing suit. It is a 4 star wonder."

Really psyched at the prospect of spending a night at a 4 star beach hotel , Massimo, Joe Zang and myself headed to Palermo for a series of meetings, knowing that after the meetings we would be able to spend an hour or two on a great Mediterranean beach.

Wrong.

After a two and a half hour drive through the west coast of Sicily, and after passing some of the most breathtaking scenery that I have seen in a long time, we hit town.

Massimo had been careful to tell Manfredi that there were three of us, and Manfredi told him that he had reserved a three-bed suite at the hotel.

Wrong.

After arriving dead tired, hot and in desperate need of a dip in the sea, we looked at the room.

One child's bed and one double bed there for 3 grown men.

When we told the clerk the problem, the clerk told us that that's it; that the hotel was completely sold out, and that is all he had.

No apology, nothing. Take it or leave it, Sicilian style.

Knowing that it was Manfredi's problem and not ours since we were his guest, and the last thing a Sicilian wants is to lose face, especially in front of very good customers, I decided to let him fix the problem.

Which he did.

Massimo ended up in a nearby hotel, Joe and I ended up in the room.

Joe, a dear friend, was on his first trip to Sicily with us. Joe had suffered a few mishaps along the way though. First, he had stubbed his toe the day before and his big toe was three times its normal size, then he had stepped into fresh concrete that the workers had poured, giving him an authentic pair of "Sicilian shoes", but most important was he was already stressed out about what his wife would say to him on his return.

You see, Joe's wife, fearful that Joe was loosing his svelte figure, has sent him to a nutritionist in June, and had admonished him to eat carefully while on this trip.

Ya, right!

The *gelato* sellers had declared a national holiday because of Joe. He had gobbled up *cornetti*, brioche and granita, pizza, pasta, risotto, and half the island of Sicily. The economy was practically humming because of him.

I actually saw him eat a little fruit and salad too, mentioning his wife's name and telling us how proud she would be seeing him eat greens and fruit.

Ya, right.

Anyway, since he was carrying a heavy load of nutritionist-guilt with him to Capo San Vito, I decided to give him the double bed and I slept on the cot.

That night, Manfredi treated us to dinner, and then Joe and Massimo disappeared again. They had found Caldo-Freddo, the best gelato joint in town and had given it a work out.

Anyway, we returned to Catania, content on a job well done. We had experienced another adventure, and our pal Joe had fallen in love with Sicilia.

Joe left Sicily three days later and I am sure that his wife has him counting calories and munching on carrots again. But I think in the back of Joe's mind it will be a long time before he forgets the delicious foods that our island offered him.

Joe is a great guy and I dear friend, and I am very happy that he had such a wonderful trip, and maybe next year we will go on another "business" (wink, wink) trip together.

As Joe said to me, "Alfred, this dinner was so good I can't wait to get hungry again!!

9. Mazara Del Vallo

Actually, I am going to tell you about an excellent adventure that you can experience when you are here.

If you have a chance, you must take a drive on highway A29 from Mazara del Vallo to Palermo.

Mazara del Vallo is located on the southwest portion of the island, Palermo to the north. Thus the trip I recommend, two hours in duration, will take you south to north.

Maraza del Vallo was under Arabic rule 1100 years ago. Today Arabic influence still permeates the area. Without a doubt, this small city rivals any in Sicily in terms of sheer beauty.

The streets are narrow and cobble-stone covered. Terra-cotta yellow and rose are the colors. Ancient statuary sit on virtually every corner.

The sea is light blue, clear. The sunlight, brilliant.

Sicilians there enjoy life, with food the centerpiece of their existence.

My law partner, Massimo, who lives in Catania, and assists me in all my endeavors here, was himself taken aback by the beauty of this area.

We went to a small pizzeria upon our arrival (believe me, there is nothing whatsoever in common with an American pizzeria and a Sicilian pizzeria, nothing). And after eating we watched as beautiful Sicilian men and woman went up to an area put aside for karaoke sing a long, and began to sing and dance.

As I watched the 100% Sicilians, dance and sing I was transported 11 centuries back in time and to the Mid-East.

Their movements were elegant, the ambiance of the moment compelling: simply unbelievable.

The next morning, Massimo and I departed this wondrous place and headed to Palermo on business.

The ride from there to Palermo rivals the scenery in the western portion of the United States, especially the Grand Canyon area.

Hugging the sea, which always was to our left, we passed spectacular valleys with majestic mountains hitting us in the face at every turn.

The farmland area, beautiful rolling hills of the most spectacular green and rust colored earth, gave a terrific juxtaposition of the Island's beauty.

Closer to Palermo loomed the breathtaking mountain called the Punta Raisi.

As we approached Palermo Airport, we stopped briefly to say a quick prayer for the two heroic judges assassinated by the Mafia a decade and a half ago.

Judge Borsellino and his wife were killed driving along this very road. Imagine an entire section of a major highway destroyed by assassins! They had placed dynamite along the highway and hitched a remote control device that killed Judge Borsellino.

Anyway, I prepared now for my visit to the most important, beautiful, magical, scary, historical and profound city in all of Sicily: Palermo.

10. Palermo: Brief History:

The city of Palermo lies in a cove known as the Conca d'Oro with a back drop of the magical Mt. Pellegrino.

Palermo is the capital city of the Autonomous Region of Sicily. The Phoenicians called it Ziz (Flower) and the Greeks called it Panormus (All Harbour).

Palermo has been inhabited since prehistoric times. It was first a Punic settlement and later a Roman colony.

From 535 to 831 it was under Byzantine rule and in 1072, it was seized by the Saracens (from modern day Libya and North Africa) who turned the city into a thriving center of commerce, agriculture and art.

Roger II wrested Palermo from the Saracens and thus began a golden period of Norman rule culminating with the rule of Frederick II (known as *Stupor Mundi* (the Wonder of the World). Under Frederick, Palermo became the center of commerce and culture in Europe, and literature, mathematics and architecture flourished.

During this period, buildings such as the Cathedral, the Palatine Chapel, The Martorana, St. John's of the Hermits, Saint Cataldo, the Zisa and Cuba were built.

It is said that these building rival any in Europe for beauty.

When the Anjevins came to power, Palermo declined in stature and fell into a dark period. The Revolt of the Vespers in 1282 expelled them from the city.

After this date, the Aragonese took possession of the city restoring it to its former prosperity. They introduced the Baroque style of architecture into Palermo, and the ancient center of the city still bears this style.

Finally in 1860, Garibaldi's Army of 1000 broke the Spanish domination which ultimately led to the unification of Italy.

Palermo is my favorite city in all Sicily. It is also a perfect example of how people of different cultures and backgrounds can live in peace and harmony. Arabs, Moroccans, Northern Italians, Greeks, French, Spanish all have blended together to create a fascinating and magical place!

11. Santo Stefano di Camastra

Massimo and I had just returned from gallivanting all over Sicily lining up deliveries for All Things Sicilian throughout the year and we had one more stop to make: Santo Stefano di Camastra.

One of my favorite pastime in Sicily is enjoying the great Sicilian scenery as we travel from place to place, especially in January, when the *autostrada* is clear of tourists and the weather is wonderful (low 60s every day).

Today we were heading to the province of Messina.

We had an appointment with our ceramic producer Collogio who owns a great ceramic factory in the little town of Santo Stefano di Camastra in the province of Messina. I really like this particular trip because that means eating at one of the hidden treasures in Sicily: Trattoria da Giannino (via Garibaldi, no. 14, tel 0921331748 trattoriadagiannino@tiscali.it).

To get to Santo Stefano from Aci San Filippo, where I live, you first have to drive north toward Messina then west toward toward Palermo. About halfway to Palermo is the exit to Santo Stefano.

I was bugging Massimo as we drove past Messina to stop by the Duomo there so I can watch the magnificent figures of its clock as they whirl and move. The clock is enormous and draws thousands of tourists every day. Massimo tried to tell me of Messina's history, but of course, his version of history differs from what actually happened. What I do know is that Messina is a city that has suffered great tragedy and destruction throughout its existence from the devastating earthquake that killed 60,000 in the early 20th century to the destruction (almost 95% was destroyed) caused by the Allies during World War II. This was the last German stronghold as the Nazis retreated from the English and Patton's Army, and believe me, the Allies pummeled them.

Anyway, we got at the Duomo at 12:30 and waited for 30 minutes until 1PM, but nothing happened. Puzzled, I stopped a passerby and asked him if the clock was broken or something. He looked at me as if I were an idiot (which, believe me, I was). "The clock chimes every day only at noon, you missed it for today," he said as he shook his head and walked away.

As usual, Massimo (who would get lost in a circle, I swear) started to laugh and said "Alfred, we will come back another time!"

After the drive to Santo Stefano and our meeting with Collogio, we walked through the town admiring its winding streets and its breathtaking panoramic view of the sea below. The cobblestone streets were a perfect juxtaposition and complement to this magnificent Sicilian paradise and its view below.

Now, we were hungry, and for the third time in the last twelve months, we had lunch at the greatest little *trattoria* in the Messina province.

The *Trattoria da Giannino* is small, seating no more than 30, but rustic. Entering that place brings you back in time to when simplicity was the way of life.

I usually start with the antipasto rustico: a plate with samples of the local antipasto, including cheeses, eggplant, peppers, meat and fish and together with a little hot bread dipped in 100% extra virgin olive oil, I go to heaven.

Massimo had the pasta special of the day: a *nidi* noodle hand made with a tomato sauce, but I chose the *nero di seppia*, the black cuttle fish sauce that sends me over the top.

Add a little *vino bianco della casa* to the offering, and for $35.00 we ate like kings.

If you are traveling thru the Messina province, circle this little treasure on the map: simply a great afternoon!

12. Lu Triangulu di la Morti

Today I started off the day by traveling Misterbianco to do a little shopping at my favorite discount brand name store, Scarringi. This store has something for everyone, except me. Since I normally wear size xxl in the states, that means here I should wear size xxxxl, which is never available. I remember one time years ago when my luggage was misplaced by Alitalia and I came to Scarringi to buy some boxers. Not knowing the size difference, I selected some nifty boxers size xxl in a package and went home and scraped off what I was wearing. I swear to God, I could not get the new ones over my knees. I pulled and pulled, and when I finally got them on, I then knew what women felt like when they had to put on a girdle. My stomach had moved mysteriously to my chest and while I looked great, I couldn't breathe. My friend who works there, Angela, as beautiful a Sicilian gal as there is, still kids me about that day. Anyway, I had no luck trying on shirts, unless I wanted to walk around with an unbuttoned shirt.

Geez.

I then headed up to the original "Triangulu di la Morti" (The Triangle of Death), the area between Misterbianco, Belpasso and Paternò that once made Iraq's Triangle of Death look like Disneyland, to see my friend Salvo who makes Sicily's best marmalade (and which I import).

Paternò is a rough and tumble town full of rough and tumble people. The guys there all wear the "coppola," the hat that De Niro wore in the *Godfather*, are generally unshaved and have cigarettes dangling from their mouths. They leave me alone, though. Last year when I was there, one guy actually has a "pistola" stuck in his waistband. I remember him looking at me and asked if I was carrying a weapon. I looked up at the sky and said to him "Predator." The guy turned white, and I guess the story got around town. In any case, I did my business with my pal Salvo and headed to Bronte, home of Europe's best pistachio growers.

Getting there is half the fun. The hills are full of fichid'india, prickly pears as we call them back in the states, and Bronte is literally a hill town. Imagine living in a place that is built on a 45 degree angle, straight down. There is not a flat space anywhere. Sometimes I think people have one leg shorter that the other because they do not seem to mind. The incline is so bad that when you park your car, not only does the emergency brake have to be engaged, but the wheel better be turned into the sidewalk too or else the car will roll all the way back to Catania. The people here are great, friendly and they do things with pistachio that are legendary. Cannoli with pistachios, pistacchio *torte, crema di pistacchio*, you name, it is made of pistachio.

Right now pistachio prices are high. The harvest takes place only every three years, and demand for these jewels is high. After conducting my business, I headed home to clean up. Traffic back is Catania was a joke. My clutch and horn was going non-stop, but hey, I am a Boston driver, so I can hang with the best of them. I finished the night by stopping by my pal Salvo's restaurant in Aci San Filippo and had a wonderful bowl of *spaghetti con nero di seppia,* that wonderful concoction of black ink squid sauce that leaves your mouth black after you eat it. Just heavenly.

Next week I have appointments all over the place. My friends from Sciacca are meeting me at the Excelsior Hotel in Catania and others from Palermo are arriving the next day. Tomorrow I will take it easy and tackle the wash. I have a small Mt. Etna of dirty clothes accumulating in my bedroom and need to find some clean boxers.

13. Siracusa

When visiting Siracusa, I suggest starting at the old section, Ortigia. There you will find its two ports, *Porto Grande* and *Porto Pico*. In ancient times both ports were important ports for the Greeks and Carthaginians, and the scene of many battles and sieges. Looking out to the Ionian Sea from the dock it is easy to imagine Greek and Phoenician ships locked in battle, or a Roman siege force. Even the sounds of ancient battle can be "heard".

We visited the ancient Greek theater where Aristophanes performed his plays, and the great Sicilian-born Greek mathematician, Archimedes, invented defensive battlements to hold off the Romans until being betrayed by a traitor who unlocked the city's gates and let the Romans inside during battle.

Archimedes was said to have invented huge mirrors that he pointed at Roman ships, and the sun's reflection set them ablaze. He was the guy who shouted "Eureka!" (Greek for "I found it!") when he was asked to certify if a present for the king was genuine gold. As I recall, he was taking a bath and he noticed that when he put too much water in the tub it overflowed. Thus he figured out water displacement and weight measurement. He was a true genius, and one of the greatest "Sicilians". Archimedes' tomb is rumored to be somewhere in the Greek Theater, and we were taken to a spot where it is believed he was buried. I remember that the stone steps of the theater were hot hot hot!

After touring downtown "modern" Siracusa with its white marble with interesting Greek and Roman architecture every place you look, we headed out of town to the countryside for our cookout with all the big shots.

Monti Iblei is the mountain chain that forms the outer perimeter of the city. The soil is among Europe's most fertile and as a matter of fact, the olives from the Buccheri area of the Iblei Mountains were so valuable that both the Greeks and later the Romans used them as currency. After parking our car in the middle of the winding countryside, we had to walk on foot down a dirt path for about one mile in order to get to the farmhouse. Upon arrival, Massimo and I looked at each other in awe. The farmhouse was a beautiful 17th century villa still completely functioning. It was set up on a hill with a 360 degree view of the countryside below. Lush lemon and olive trees dotted the countryside and the smell of the barbeque hit our noses.

We feasted that night. Authentic sausage, peppers, tomatoes as big as a basketball that were succulent as any that I have ever eaten. Pizza baked in an outdoor wood fired oven, fish grilled on an outdoor stone, mouthwatering desserts and vino, plenty of vino. Anyway, we ate and hob-nobbed with the Siracusan elite that night. It was a wondrous and fun filled night to be sure. By the time we had to leave, we had to retrace our walk on the dirt path to find our car and then drive out of the *campagna* with zero street lights to guide our way! Massimo was going crazy as he was driving and cursing the Sicilian road builders.

It was a wonderful experience for both of us an evening I will never forget, Siracusan hospitality at its best!

14. Tindari

Before I left for Sicily in December, Tim (one of our regular customers) contacted me and asked if I had ever been to Tindari. He mentioned that he always wanted a statue of the fabled Black Madonna at the Sanctuary of the Madonna (Santuario Maria ss Madonna) located high in the mountaintop village of Tindari.

Always looking for new adventure, Massimo and I decided that we could divert time from our busy schedule to find a statue for Tim. My girlfriend was with us on this trip. Olga, a native of St. Petersburg, Russia is an art expert. Over the years we have visited some of the finest museums and art galleries in Europe, and she was eager to visit the Sanctuary as she had heard many stories of its beauty. So, on a warm January morning, with camera in hand, we set out to find the Black Madonna.

Tindari is located off the Messina-Palermo *autostrada* (exit Nazionale 113) about an hour from our starting point, Messina. With Massimo at the wheel, after exiting the highway, as usual, we got lost. I often joke that if Massimo were Columbus, the earth would be flat, and I am not too far off when I say that! Anyway, after asking directions several times, and climbing a small mountain, we parked the car and headed toward the Sanctuary.

Tindari is an ancient village, founded by the Greeks in the fourth century B.C. Over the centuries it has experienced periods of great magnificence, but also terrible suffering, especially during the Saracen occupation. During the first century AD, Christianity flourished, but as various tyrants came to power, Christians were persecuted. Tindari did not escape the anguish.

In 726AD, Sanctuary of Tindari, emperor of the East and a pagan, issued an edict forbidding the adoration of any form of statue and ordered the destruction of all statues. In an effort to hide their statues, the residents of sea towns would entrust them to sailors who would hide them on their ships.

Legend has it that one such ship from the east carried a hidden chest containing the figure of the Madonna. It was forced to seek harbor in the Bay of Tindari-Marinello because of a terrible storm on the Tyrrhenian Sea. Once the storm was over, the ship would not move because it was stuck in the sand, and the sailors were forced to empty the ship in an effort to lighten its load. When they unloaded the chest containing the Madonna and opened it, they were stunned with its beauty. They placed the statue on the hill of Ceres, the location of a temple dedicated to Ceres, the goddess of the harvest. News spread fast throughout the population about the arrival of this strange and mysterious statue, and soon thousands were flocking to Tindari to pray to the Madonna and ask for her mercy.

The statue is wooden and parts have been carved (face, hands and feet). The remainder of the body is covered with a red tunic and a dark blue cloak embroidered with golden stars. Presently the Madonna is covered by a silk mantle and she wears a crown placed above an oriental tunic. Her complexion is olive-black. The sculpture is Byzantine in style and she is depicted holding the Holy Infant in her lap. In 1544, the first sanctuary was built, but destroyed soon after by Algerian pirates. In 1598 it was rebuilt. As time wore on and devotion to the Madonna increased, the tiny sanctuary was replaced by a larger sanctuary. In 1956 construction began on a sanctuary which was completed in 1963. It was consecrated by Cardinal Salvatore Pappalardo on May 1, 1979.

Our mouths dropped as we gazed at the beautiful sanctuary and the Madonna. Olga was moved, commenting on the solemnity of the setting. It was absolutely breathtaking. Set above the nave of the altar in resplendent array, sat the Madonna. The daily Mass was being offered, and I was struck by the fervor of prayer that the faithful exhibited. Near the front entrance of the sanctuary a statue shop was run by the nuns who take care of the church. We purchased a beautiful statue for our friend, Tim, (I had never seen a nun use a credit card machine before: another first for me!) and I carried the statue on my lap back to the States. Tindari, another of the countless treasures of my Island. Do you think that Tim will like the statue? I do.

Chapter Twenty-Seven

1. Prelude: Unity with the Soil.

Prelude: Unity with the soil.
I have blisters on my hands and my shoulder is killing me.
It is the most pleasant pain that I have experienced in years.
Why?
For the last few hours, I have been working the Sicilian soil, raking, pulling weeds, doing landscaping on the new villa.

As the hot Sicilian sun beats on my body and as sweats drips from my brow, I think of two men who once did the same thing as I: my grandfathers Alfio Zappalà and Gaetano Torrisi.

They too once worked the soil here, toiling in the hills of Trecastagni as teenagers, working as laborers for the rich vegetable growers of Catania.

I take a handful of the fertile soil and put it to my nose.

The bouquet is intoxicating, rich, fertile: the bounty of Etna,

As my back aches and the sweat blinds my vision, I work harder, faster….the sun beats on my naked torso….

Here I am in America I pay people to do exactly what I am doing, killing myself and loving every second of it.

I stop to admire my work: five huge mounds of clippings ready to be removed: only another 15 or so and my work will be done.

The sun is hot. I have visions of millennia of workers toiling the fields. Strangely, I feel a connection, a spiritual connection with them today.

Yes, I love the pain, the blisters. On Wednesday I will go to the Piano Fiori, the garden center and choose two trees, maybe a fig tree this year. I am not sure yet.

Then I will labor again, planting in the beloved soil what countless spirits now departed once did.

The hot Sicilian sun heals the spirit, I think.

2. Return to the Soil……..After 85 Years!

In many ways, throughout life I have been blessed. The Good Lord blessed me with three beautiful children (and soon a grandchild!), many wonderful friends, rich cultural experiences and the gift of painting a picture with words.

Let me tell you about another gift received in May while on my Sicilian adventure. As many of you know, I have a wonderful villa in Aci San Filippo, not far away from Acireale.

Upon arrival in Sicily, I always spend the first few days trying to fix up the villa a little more adding or changing this or that, or moving something from here to there. This trip, however, one project was in mind: to plant some trees in memory of my three patron saints — Alfio, Filadelfo and Cirino — in my front yard.

Thus, on a warm sunny day in early May, I visited *Piano fiore* (a garden center), not knowing what type of trees to buy. Entering the garden center, everything exotic lay before my eyes. I imagined a tropical paradise: palm trees, flowers already bursting with sweet scents, everything that even a person with the blackest of thumbs (such as I) could want.

"It's a far cry from the garden center at Home Depot," I thought. "Maybe I can actually grow something that won't die in two days."

The clerk was very helpful. I explained to him what I wanted, and Stefano (by now he was my friend) fell all over me with kindness.

Five trees were selected: lemon, orange, olive, mandarin, and bergamot. A couple of trips back and forth to the villa and, presto, they were in the yard ready for planting. After finding a store that sold rakes and shovels, the planting began.

"Alfred," Stefano had advised, "don't forget to place the trees four meters apart." "Water them twice a day for two weeks until they take."

The shovel was placed in the ground and as the first shovel full of earth was turned, something hit me. I thought of my grandfathers, Gaetano Torrisi and Alfio Zappalà, both long departed, who left Sicily 85 years ago as teenagers to go to America in search for a better life.

Both loved the Three Saints while they were alive. As a matter of fact, my grandfather Gaetano was one of the organizers of the Feast of the Three Saints in Lawrence, Massachusetts; today, the Labor Day Weekend festival there is one of the biggest festivals in New England, drawing 100,000 people annually.

As sweat poured from my forehead under the hot Sicilian sun, I felt them looking over my shoulder, smiling at me. Both would approve of my project. If alive, both would be supervising.

The earth was dark brown, rich and fertile. Taking a handful near my nose I smelled its fragrance, a bouquet I will never forget.

Its essence will be remembered and recalled every time I am stuck in a New England snowstorm.

One by one the trees went up. The lemon tree I named Alfio; the orange tree, Filadelfo; the olive tree, Cirino.

As I was finishing planting, Massimo stopped by. "Alfred," he said, "you are crazy. You will hurt yourself. Let me call the landscapers to finish for you."

This was one task, however, I was intent on completing myself. Hours passed as I dug. Sweat streamed from every pore. I dug and dug. My back ached. Finally, all five were planted, each straight, each majestic. A sense of accomplishment overwhelmed me. I felt like a kid again.

Over the next couple of days, I planted some nice flowers and bushes too. The remaining two trees I named after Massimo and me. There was a reason for this: I will return July 17th for the baptism of Massimo's new baby, Marzio.

Another beautiful spot is picked out on another level of the villa where two more trees will be planted. These trees will be extra special. They will be called Gaetano and Alfio: two fig trees, symbolic of Sicily and trees that both of my grandfathers grew and enjoyed in America. Those trees will become my favorites too. I think of my grandfathers often and now they will never be forgotten.

On May 9 and 10, I attended the Feast of the Three Saints in Trecastagni. As the statues of St. Alfio were being carried out of the church, I think I saw him smile at me.

3. Aftermath: Visiting an Old Friend

Four years ago, I remember laboring under the hot Sicilian sun one July afternoon as I planted a small sapling olive tree in my old house. The little guy was about twelve inches high when I dug that fertile earth and planted him as sweat rolled down my face. I remembered my two grandfathers that day and wondered if they had planted anything in the wonderful soil ninety years ago before they departed for America. Somehow, planting that tree connected me to them. When I moved to Acitrezza two years later, I was told that the tree, which was then about two feet high, could not be pulled up and replanted as there was no adequate space in my new place for it to grow. Reluctantly, I left that tree that I had planted, but promised myself that when I return to Sicily I would drop by that old house and pay it a visit.

Yesterday, I did. He's four feet tall now, double the size since last year. He is a handsome fellow now: strong trunk with many branches. He has come a long way these last four years. I pulled the car over and gazed at my tree. Somehow, I felt better about this situation. Now it seems I have contributed something to Sicily. Perhaps it is a small, insignificant gift. After all, Sicily has many thousands olive trees, but to me I was happy that something that I did has become part of the permanent Sicilian landscape.

Call me sentimental, call me an old fool, but I bet my two grand-fathers, Alfio Zappalà and Gaetano Torrisi were watching over that tree and sending it water every once in a while. At my new place, I planted some cactus and herbs in the flower pots on my decks. Maybe one or two of those guys will last, too. I hope so.

Chapter Twenty-Eight

You'd Think I'd Learn!

The Mighty Sicilian *Crispelle*. Have you ever eaten a *crispelle*?

I am talking about those fried dough type of things that are stuffed either with anchovies, ricotta cheese or are "plain" covered with sugar.

Yup, those delectable delights that go straight to your stomach and sit there all day long and if you are an old geezer like me, are a cause to reach for the Zantac later in the day.

Why oh why do I subject myself to the yearly torture of eating about six of those bombs at one sitting and then spending the rest of the day regretting that I did that?

Well, because I love them, that's why.

Labor Day weekend is the time to munch these things and for me the local Feast of The Three Saints in Lawrence, MA is the place.

In Sicily I tried eating them several times, but the pain was too much. Instead of frying these little indigestion creators in a decent trans fatty acid free oil, the Sicilians fry them in lard: old fashioned dead animal fat, and these things are intestine killers for sure.

My fried Peter makes them here in the states. He has been doing it for a long time and is the "maestro" of the *crispelle*.

Yesterday I had my annual allotment and for the rest of the weekend I will pay the price.

Why, Alfred, do you do this to yourself every year? Why don't you adopt a healthy lifestyle and just say no?

Are you nuts?

Eating them has been a right of passage for almost six decades now. Why, a year without a *crispelle* would be like them canceling Christmas, for Pete's sake.

Nope! I will keep munching these things and suffer every year.

Some people will never learn.

Then again, why learn?

Chapter Twenty-Nine

Perpetual Rebirth

It was the smell and the color of the wild flowers that first got to me. I cannot imagine that springtime flowers can be more fragrant or blossom more beautifully than they do in Sicily. The shades and subtle hues of pinks, yellow, and reds are an artist's Nirvana.

Driving up the mountain roads to Etna for the first time accompanied by my cousin, Tom Torrisi, and his wife, Marianne, was an unforgettable experience. The sun was warm as we piled into the tiny, four seater car. The pristine air was perfumed with the springtime fragrance of an island in bloom. We planned to loop the mountain from our oceanside starting point at the Hotel Sant'Andrea in order to explore the Sicilian countryside towns of Randazzo, Belpasso, Adrano, Misterbiance, and Paternò, then head south to glimpse at Acireale, Acicastello and Acitrezza.

Throwing off the dreary New England winter doldrums was our primary objective, removing ourselves from the oppressive, black end-of-winter snow. Springtime in Sicily is genuinely a remedy for whatever ails you. Driving up and down the country roads, the war, the economy, the everyday stresses of American life rapidly become a distant memory. One is transported back to a bygone era, one of simplicity and naivety, borne of sorrow and heartache, yet a place where you become one with Mother Earth. An example of constant rebirth.

The sweeping panoramas and breathtaking vistas, are blurred by recollection of the tragedy of this country's historic background. Wars, tragedies and occupation by European countries robbed the country of her treasure, her life. I wonder at her ability to renew herself, to heal and nourish all, despite the terrible afflictions that have befallen her throughout the centuries. Sicily has survived countless calamities: earthquakes, volcanic eruptions, Nazi occupation, Spanish occupation, the list goes on. Amazingly, all is forgotten and forgiven.

The sweet fragrance of the field poppies fills my nostrils. The warm sun heals my spirit. The Lord now lives here. Over the years, many with whom I have traveled return to the States, changed individuals. By discovering where they came from they re-discover who they are. Sicily is the elixir for the soul. Sicily in the spring. a juxtaposition of past, present and future, an embodiment of the trials and tribulations of life, and the spirit of survival, a tribute to man and his indomitable spirit, to the universe, and the confluence of the two.

Remarkable, how the simple fragrance of Spring blossoms opens the remote corners of the mind. Such is Sicily's gift to us.

Chapter Thirty

My Town

1. Hither and Yon!

I got an early start this morning and headed to Trecastagni, my ancestral hometown and took part in the annual Festa di Sant'Alfio, a thousand year old festival that honors the three brothers Alfio, Cirino and Filadelfo who were martyred by the Romans for refusing to give up their Christian faith. This is one of Sicily's biggest festivals (Sant'Agata in Catania and Santa Rosalia in Palermo are bigger, but hey, Trecastagni has a population of 8,000 that swells to 4,0000 for this festival.

The festival started last evening with one of Sicily's biggest fireworks displays, far bigger than Boston's Fourth of July fireworks display, except that it takes place about 300 feet over your head. Now I know what the bombing of Fort Sumner felt like. Totally awesome. Set to music, too.

This morning started with the March of the "carretti," those beautiful horses all decked out with colorful plumes of feathers and pulling the Sicilian cart full of people playing the "friscaletti" and having a truly wonderful time. About fifty carts took part this year and the people (all 40,000 of them) really enjoyed themselves. BTW: If you go to You Tube and search Festa Sant'Alfio Trecastagni Sicily, you can watch the best parts. I later swung by the Church of Sant'Alfio, which has around the clock masses going for three days, and placed one of those giant votive candles in memory of my mom, dad, and grandparents in the area where thousands of candles were burning. It is always a very special and emotional moment for me, and I have made now this annual pilgrimage since 1997. Grazie a Dio.

After returning to my car (I know now where to park to avoid traffic), I headed to the *Autostrada* and twenty minutes later I exited at the "Taormina Mare" turn-off. I parked my car at the municipal lot and took the "Funivia" tram up to the town. I love walking up the main street, Corso Umberto, bubbling with activity, shops all over the place. I headed to my favorite place, the Wunderbar: an outdoor café in the Piazza April IX, surrounded by the most breathtaking view of Naxos Bay 3000 feet below and mighty Etna lurking right in front of my face.Simply, there is no finer view anywhere. I ordered what I always order at the Wunderbar: *granita di mandorla* (almond granita), an espresso, and a bottle of water. For the next two hours, I watched people from all walks of life pass by. This year, Taormina is loaded with Germans, English, Russians, and Chinese. Very few Americans, although I did chat with a couple from North Carolina who were passing thru town. I also bumped into a nice couple who had driven down to Lawrence several months back to ask me what they should do in Sicily on their honeymoon. Taking my suggestion, they both thanked me profusely as they said they were having the time of their life. I was amazed that I had bumped into them.

At seven PM, I headed back to the villa, but on the way home at Centro Squalo, the large supermarket that has everything in it now and bought some fresh calamari which was swimming in the ocean earlier in the day. A little olive oil, a squeeze of two lemons, and a hot grill later, I was one happy camper.

Tonight I will sit on my deck and break open that bottle of Sicilian DOP wine that I have been saving. The night is warm, the sea is calm, the moon is brilliant, and my IPOD is all charged up. Tonight I will listen to Dave Matthews.

I ask you: what can be better?

Ciao!

2. The Miracle in Lawrence

I am not much of a miracle guy. I probably am a descendant of the original "Show me" guy, Saint Thomas and should live in the "Show me" state of Missouri. However, now I have to believe.

Here's the story:

Back about 90 years ago, my grandfather Gaetano Torrisi and a group of faithful immigrants from Sicily helped form The Sant'Alfio Society in Lawrence, Massachusetts, named for the three young boys Alfio, Filadelfo and Cirino who were tortured and killed by the Romans sixteen centuries ago for refusing to give up their faith.

For centuries, the Feast of Sant'Alfio has been celebrated in Sicily, especially in the mountain towns of Trecastagni, Pedara, Sant'Alfio and south in Lentini.

When my grandfather and the others came to America, they brought with them the Feast.

Roughly 80 years ago (some say now even longer), the first few Festivals were held by them. As the years passed and more immigrants arrived, the festival grew larger and larger.

After moving from one meeting place to another over the decades, they settled into a small meeting hall adjacent to the Holy Rosary Church, on Common Street in Lawrence, the very street where arriving Sicilian immigrants settled initially.

The Feast of the Three Saints, as it is now called, is held every year over Labor Day weekend and draws nearly 100,000 people from far and wide.

Back when my grandfather was involved, it was an event for families to gather and adore the Three Saints. However, it was held over the Labor Day weekend instead of May 9-10 as it is in Sicily because that is when even the sweatshops of Lawrence gave their workers a day off.

If you do not know about Lawrence, its garment and shoe sweat shops back then ultimately led to the Great Strike of 1912, now known as the Bread and Roses Strike, and as a result child-labor laws were enacted as well as general working condition laws for the workers. Some say that the American Labor Movement was founded that day.

Prior to that time, immigrants worked in inhumane conditions for slave wages, children too.

However, every year, the "Festa di Sant'Alfio" was the one weekend that Sicilian immigrants from the Mount Etna Region (primarily those from Trecastagni, Pedara, Sant'Alfio, Catania, Lentini, and a few other mountain towns) could celebrate the martyrdom of the three brothers, Alfio, Cirino and Filadelfo who were put to death in the Third Century AD.

The love that the old timers brought with them for the Three Saints was passed down from generation to generation, from grandfather to father to son.

Thus, the passion remains burning hot, after all these years.

However, this year will be very special. Here's why:

Last year, right after the Feast was over, the old building, which housed the statues of the Three Saints as well as served as a meeting place for the members, was torn down.

It was old, tired and had served the faithful well.

The tiny group of members, roughly 150 (from this number a substantial number are elderly, thus the actual "working number" of members is far less), decided to raise money and build a new building on the footprint of the old building.

Some were concerned that in this economy asking for donations for such a huge project would be futile. Others were concerned that it could never be built in time for this year's Feast.

They were wrong on both counts.

Miraculously, money poured in from all over. Donations from $5.00 or $10.00 to larger donations in the hundreds and thousands of dollars.

The call went out and the faithful heeded that call.

This tiny "band of brothers" not only raised the money with raffles, by scouring far and wide for monetary contributors, by having various fundraisers, but once the money was raised, they worked night and day to build a gleaming new building, which resembles the original church of Sant'Alfio in Trecastagni in 10 months!

On August 23rd, the new building will be dedicated, two weeks before the Feast!

These "heroes" worked tirelessly on this project, day and night for nine months, planning, ripping, tearing, supervising, worrying, lifting, hammering, painting and they did it!

Two weeks ahead of schedule and in time for the Labor Day weekend celebration!

I consider this a miracle.

Many immigrant families in this area, their sons, daughters, grandsons and granddaughters, all moved by the spirit of the Three Saints and their own families put their collective spirits and will together to accomplish this miracle.

My boyhood friend Wayne Peters (his mother is a Larratonda) as President of the Society led a crew of diehards on this task.

I will not name the others as they know who they are and that is all that really matters. But all of them gave willing, lovingly, wholeheartedly, night and day for this project.

I know that the Three Saints today are looking down from heaven and are smiling.

After 1600 years, the faithful still believe and now their descendants have made it possible for future generations to learn and believe too.

The Miracle in Lawrence happened.

I know. I saw it with my own eyes.

3. The Connection

My grandfathers (both of them) Gaetano Torrisi and Alfio Zappalà came from Trecastagni which is nestled in the foothills of Etna just above Catania.

Like most Sicilians, they came to the USA shortly after the tragic influenza outbreak of 1908 which killed tens of thousands. As Ireland had its Potato Famine of the late 1800's which caused mass Irish emigration to the USA, the influenza outbreak in the early 20th century was one of the major reasons for the mass exodus from Sicily by many Sicilian immigrants.

My grandfathers told me the story of the three young boys, aged 21, 20, and 18, Alfio, Cirino and Filadelfo, who were martyred by the Romans for refusing to give up their Christian faith 1700 years ago.

Sent to Sicily from Rome by the authorities in an attempt to get them to deny their Christian faith, the boys landed in Messina and were bound, beaten, tortured, and brought to the village of Sant'Alfio, then on to Trecastagni where they rested and continued to Lentini where they were further tortured and finally put to death.

The historical record has documented thousands of miracles by the faithful who have asked their intercession.

Trecastagni means "three chaste lambs" named after the three saints. A must see is the Church of Sant'Alfio. Inside the Church of Sant'Alfio is the "Hall of Miracles" containing hundreds of attestations by those who prayed to the Saints in their time of need and whose prayers were answered. A walk through The Hall of Miracles will truly move you.

I have made pilgrim ages to the Feast every year for the last 6 years and I never seem to get over the zeal, love and fervor people from all over Sicily have for these three saints.

Last year at the Feast I met a delegation of 40 Australians who came to celebrate. They told me that the Feast is also celebrated in Australia!

Of course, in Lawrence, Massachusetts, The Feast of the Three Saints celebrated over Labor Day weekend is the biggest Italian-American event in New England attracting tens of thousands.

In Sicily, the Feast now rivals the February Feast of Saint Agatha in popularity,(although that feast in Catania is much bigger).

During the Trecastagni festival the sidewalks are chock full of vendors selling everything imaginable from shoes and suits to furniture, dinnerware, and clothing of all types.

Last year for $4,00 I bought an espresso coffee pot that sells for $20.00 here in the States.

Hint: if you go there be careful of what you eat! I was told after I ate a "delicious" steak sandwich that it was really horse meat!

However, other food vendors have wondrous fare including pasta, *granite, cornetti con crema, gelato, paste di mandorla* and many other delicious treats!

May is a wonderful month weather-wise as everything is in bloom with the strawberry crop being the first harvested. Other delicious fruits also are sold by countless roadside vendors.

If you have to pick a month to go away, I suggest now is the time!

Chapter Thirty-One

Arrivals

1. Sicily….Blowing in the Wind!

A complete monsoon. Howling winds. No heat. No internet. Rain far worse that anything Noah had to contend with.

This is the background of my arrival in Sicily.

I left Boston the night of the 25th, with IPOD in hand and flew in Amsterdam via Northwest. After a brief layover, I continued to Rome where I spent four hours enjoying myself there before continuing on to Catania.

I recommend an IPOD for travel. My sister gave one to me for Christmas along with my very favorite music. Believe me, there is nothing more enjoyable that walking the airport in Rome with Bonnie Raitte singing a love song to you, especially during the holiday season.

It was a truly enjoyable trip over here.

Then the rains came. Mamma Mia, what rains!

I picked up my car and in a torrential downpour drove to Acitrezza on the shore road, heading to my new condo.

Massimo did a great job moving everything over from the old place for me, but I had to de-box things and put them away.

Just the sort of thing one wants to do after a 15 hour trip.

Anyway, I flopped on the bed and noticed that the place was cold. No heat. I switched the system on and off, but nothing. Bundling up with sweaters and blankets, I figured that I would call the gas company the next day to check out the problem.

The next morning, after knocking the icicles off my body and scraping the frost from the bathroom mirror, I called the gas company. Surprisingly, they came within two hours.

Sebastiano, the repair man, told me that he needed to get a part for the heating unit, but he could get the hot water going. However, I would be without heat for two more days until the part came in.

To make a long story short, I froze my keester off, and I think I peed ice cubes there for a while.

Thankfully, the heat was restored yesterday, and I am one happy camper today. The rain stopped last night too, and it is actually beginning to look like Sicily again, and not New England!

The condo is terrific and very comfortable now that the heat is working. It can sleep six comfortably and eight uncomfortably, although four people would be ideal. I worked on the place for two days and organized everything, even buying new wall hangings. I wanted color on the walls so I chose an African motif for the entrance, the stairs, the guest bedroom and the tv room, and I am very happy with the result.

The walls came alive, and the place now looks terrific.

I will take photos as soon as the sun comes out and post them on our website for you to look at, but really, the place is awesome.

I still have no computer service (allegedly, the service man will stop by tomorrow), so I am at an internet cafe in Acireale typing away right now. Worse case is that I will come again tomorrow and do my work here.

My dear friend and business partner Donnamarie arrived in Taormina yesterday (she coordinates the Italian language program at Babilinia School for Americans who wish to study Italian in a wonderful setting), and I hope to hook up with her for espresso or cappuccino soon.

In the meantime, I am driving the neighborhood and learning where to shop, where to eat, where to buy bread etc., and my new place is about eight miles from the old place.

This I know: People will love my new place. Once I get everything fixed, that is!

2. Another Arrival

After spending four glorious days in Rome for Christmas, on December 28th we took the short one hour flight and landed in Catania. It's funny how I experience a rebirth emotionally, physically and intellectually every time my feet hit the tarmac at Fontanarossa Airport in Catania.

Zipping from the airport to my villa, I opened the door and was inundated with a feeling of finally coming home.

Several folks rented the villa in my absence, and all left gifts of appreciation. One bought an American coffee maker from the nearby Naval Base PX. Another stocked the liquor cabinet. While another left a wonderful note and bottle of wine thanking me for a magical time using the villa. Full of appreciation and joy, the only thing left for me to do was stock the fridge.

We shop at Le Zagare in San Giovanni La Punta. It's a large shopping market similar to a Whole Foods that has two levels...on the first level is an enormous grocery market with wonderful fruits, meats, fishes and pantry items. An escalator allowing you to put your fully loaded shopping cart onto it leads you to the second level which is a department store selling everything imaginable from clothing, dry goods and electronics to books, cd's and computers. Back on the first level we did our shopping, picking our fresh fish, meat and vegetables from the different departments while sampling all sorts of fabulous delights along the way.

I have one of those cards that you present at the check-out to get points that can be later traded in for free gifts. I was happy to use it. Now I have 600 points, almost enough for a coffee cup! By the way, at the checkout you must bag your own groceries (a lot of folks bring their own canvas bags or you can buy them for 10 cents a piece at check-out).

Once our house was fully stocked with food, (we ate in every night this time because I had some killer recipes I wanted to try out using REAL Sicilian ingredients) we headed to Taormina to celebrate and photograph the New Year's Eve festivities there.

Taormina, as usual, was magnificent! This time of the year made it even more so and I highly recommend if you ever get the opportunity to visit Taormina on New Year's Eve day and experience the ambiance please do!

Musicians lined the walkways playing violins on the main piazza, while store windows were aglow with spectacular displays. Sicilian families with children were walking hand in hand up and down Corso Umberto, eating gelato and enjoying themselves.

We enjoyed stopping for an espresso and watching hundreds of happy families parade by us getting ready to ring in the New Year. At midnight it was as if a war had broken out, as from every direction we heard the sounds of fireworks and looked up to experience the beautiful explosions of color filling the sky.

New Year's Day was just as special. Massimo and Anna invited us to their house that day and, as you can imagine, Anna prepared us a traditional Sicilian New Year's day meal: antipasto and cheeses for starters, two pasta dishes (one red, one white) and both pesce spada (sword fish) and *polpette al limone* (hamburg meatballs cooked on a lemon leaf). The wine and champagne flowed as we rang in the New Year Sicilian style.

Of course, we still had one more holiday to prepare for: January 6th, The Epiphany and La Befana (which celebrates the Magi adoring the Christ child and the old woman *La Befana* still looking for the Christ child.)

January 6 is a national holiday in Sicily, so we repeated the whole thing again with Anna and Massimo except this time we also exchanged small gifts.

I am glad I got to experience the Christmas season in both Rome and Sicily. Two years ago I was there for Easter and the year before that for Thanksgiving; however, next year I will return for Christmas and possibly my brand new grand daughter Rose will be there with me too, I hope!

3. Next Time I Will Swim There!

Alitalia. Cursed words if I ever heard them.

I made it back (sadly) but not until Alitalia had another two hour delay in Rome.

This is the last time on that airline for me.

Alitalia is a textbook example of a company driven into the ground by greedy workers who care not one whit about the customers.

Thankfully, they have been sold and I hope that the black eye caused by their incompetence and mean spirits will be replaced by Air One, who purchased their assets and which is expected to start as the new entity next week.

However, I spoke to many travelers who had their vacations ruined because of the airline.

One couple (actually three couples) were enraged at the airport because their connecting flight was cancelled, which caused them to miss a connecting flight to Nice, France where they were to leave on a boat cruise. As a result, they missed the ship.

Another couple has spent the whole week in Rome with the same clothes that had arrived. Alitalia had lost their luggage.

Another couple got stranded in Malta for three days because of flight cancellations.

Never again.

From now on, I am traveling on Northwest. They have a flight from Boston to Amsterdam, then from Amsterdam to Catania. Or Luftwaffe. They have a fight from Boston to Hamburg, then Hamburg to Catania. Or Air France. They go Boston-Paris, Paris to Catania. Or I will fly on the back of a crow if necessary, not Alitalia.

Really, really bad.

That said, I am glad to be back, as we are all hopeful that the Christmas season will be at least decent for us this year.

At All Things Sicilian, we have cut pricing dramatically, knowing full well that people do not have disposable income this year. We selected items that people will enjoy at great prices, and the store is fully stocked.

Hopefully, someone will come and buy this stuff now.

Anyway, for today I will rest up bit, eat some turkey, and will be at the store every day from now until Christmas (when I leave again).

Happy Thanksgiving!

4. Holding My Breath

I arrived in Sicily after a tough 18 hour trip. Never again on Alitalia. Seems that they are striking on a whim now since the merger with Air One two months ago.

Most troubling of all though is the complete lack of remorse the staff has for travelers.

As an experienced traveler, I didn't mind the four hour layover in either Boston or Rome, but I do mind the way they treated other travelers who were traveling for the first time.

One party of six was in tears. They were on their way to Barcelona from America. Alitalia first diverted them from Madrid to Rome, then cancelled the Rome-Madrid flight.

Their once in a lifetime vacation now in ruins.

I made it safe and sound. I picked up the car and drove to the villa. Weary from such a long flight, I showered and went to Massimo's house for dinner with Massimo, Anna and the children. I had gone to Kids Gap before I left to buy the kids jackets and pajamas, warm New England stuff unavailable in Sicily, and they loved the gifts.

As usual, Anna (the most beautiful woman in Sicily, I swear) made us a great meal and I then retired back to my villa and crashed and burned.

However, my friend August, who used the villa several months ago, hung a big New York Giants banner as a welcoming present to me! I am a Patriots fan, of course. Wait until I see him!

Today, (Sunday) I was invited to Maria Pace's house for Sunday dinner with the whole family. The dinner alone was worth the trip! Tonight I am organizing the villa a bit and plan on hitting the rack early. Tomorrow I will tell you about the new place I checked out today too in Acicastello. I think I am going to move there over Christmas. Truly a special place!

God, I love Sicily. I am home.

5. Leaving (or Coming) on a Jet Plane

I left America exhausted and after a long, cold winter of discontent. Business is in shatters, and my personal life is in complete disarray, so I was looking forward to getting re-nourished back in Sicily. The departure date couldn't come fast enough, believe me.

At Logan, I noticed a big change with Alitalia. First of all, the name Air One now takes the place of Alitalia. The clerks at check in were cheerful and helpful; not like the grumpy clerks of old.

The departure was only fifteen minutes late too, through no fault of Air One. The plane clean, the atmosphere completely different. On board were very nice flight attendants: all young in their twenties and thirties who greeted people and were helpful.

Most surprising of all, the on board meal was eatable. Before when you had a choice of meat or fish, the meat was chicken and the fish was unknown. Here, the beef was real meat and tasty too.

After an eight hour flight which was smooth and efficient, we landed at Rome.

My connecting flight to Sicily was only sixty minutes later, a certainty in the past that I would catch the flight but my bags wouldn't. However, to my shock upon arrival, on the carousel were my bags.

Honestly, I was very impressed. I was impressed with the cost too. This round trip flight had cost me only $551.00. In the past, I had paid up to $1,500.00 for a ticket, so I got a great ride for a cheap price.

When I picked up my car at Hertz (again three weeks cost me exactly $624.00, 50% less than normal), to my surprise I had been upgraded from a Ford Focus to a Fiat 500: a neat little car (except that the color was yellow).

Anyway, I arrived safe and sound, had a great flight and a nifty car with a full tank of gas.

The healing began upon arrival. The weather was warm, about 75 or so, the sunshine brilliant. My spirit was being repaired, refreshed by the second.

As I headed for the *autostrada* on the way to my condo, I said a prayer of thanks. I was saved.

Chapter Thirty Two

Departures

1. The Last Lamb Chop

I have a tough decision today. Since this is really my last day here (tomorrow will spent saying my goodbyes, finishing packing, doing last minute laundry etc.), and since I never eat a big meal prior to flying, today is the last day to eat something decent.

Do I eat lamb chops and mushrooms at Piccolo Mondo again? Do I eat *nero di seppia* in Acitrezza again? Do I head up to Roberto's in Naxos and eat the best pizza in Sicily again? Or do I take a chance and go somewhere else and try to pick something off the menu that may or may not please my soul?

Decisions, decisions.

One last meal. This is the one that will linger in the memory. The choice must be exact, precise. Breakfast is no problem. Today I will have one last *cornetto con crema* instead of a brioche. That decision has been made.

For lunch, I will probably go for a small serving of *pasta al forno* (baked macaroni) at Urna's. For three euros and fifty cents, it is a no brainer.

If I eat that at lunch, it eliminates the *nero di seppia.* I never ever eat pasta twice in the same day. As a matter of fact, I usually do not eat pasta after 6:00 PM. Thus, Acitrezza is out.

Now, it looks like it is between lamb chops and pizza. Hmmm. The decision is beginning to come into view here. Pizza I can have anytime, really. However, where can I find lamb from Mt. Etna in the states?

I need to think long and hard on this one.

In any case, yesterday was my son Matt's birthday. He was 33 years old yesterday. Matt is my son, but also my best friend. He is a lawyer for the FAA, and a self made man. He recently celebrated his fourth wedding anniversary with his wife Meister, and they have two of the world's most beautiful children, Noey and little Matt.

I adore him and his family as well as my other kids Jen and Catie, and my other grand kids Rose and John. Why, I even love my son in law JR.

The tug between them and Sicily is enormous. When I move here next year, I will be making frequent trips across the big pond to see them and vice versa.

Thus, while I saddened to leave Sicily yet again, I look forward to seeing the essence of my life.

I will console myself by editing all my writings this summer into book form. I will re-live my many adventures here. I will smile and I will cry a bit. The vignettes of this place are secure in my memory: they always are.

Thus, while writing this piece, the sizzle of the lamb chop wins. The smell, taste, and after glow are too intoxicating to overcome. I am powerless to make an informed decision.

Tonight, I eat the noble lamb of Etna and toast all my paesani there.

One last thing I will do is get a haircut here. That is art of my pre-departure check list. I will visit Alfio and he will buzz cut what is left of my hair.

My August wardrobe is clean, pressed and ready for my return. Now, I am ready to return to America and face the problems there that have accumulated. Now I am ready.

However, I will be "more ready" after tonight's dinner! Over and Out: Last transmission, for now!

2. Pre-Partum Depression and the Brioche

Thankfully, in Sicily there are no Denny's Restaurants. Neither are there Al's Diner, or Joe's Greasy Spoon.

The fried egg, the bagel, bacon, pancakes, doughnuts, maple syrup, and American breakfasts in general are almost non-existent here. At the American Naval Base at Sigonella right outside Catania you can find (maybe) an American breakfast, or maybe in a five star hotel something that vaguely resembles an American breakfast MAY exist, but why bother?

Here, mornings are for glorifying and paying homage to the mighty brioche.

The brioche. That simple food that purifies the soul. Back home, we call them a sweet roll or maybe a Portuguese sweet roll. Back home, everyone I have ever tasted stinks. Awful. Terrible.

Here, eating a brioche is almost religious, a rite that is not taken lightly. Eating one, you become part of the fabric of Italy, a communion of spirit with other Italians. The brioche is the ham and egg, the pancake, the bagel, the doughnut of Italy except here it means something. It is that period of the day that energizes the soul.

The brioche can be eaten simply with an espresso or a cappuccino. The "quickie" breakfast. I have the same breakfast here every morning: Brioche, cappuccino, and a granita (half almond, half coffee, *mandorla e caffé*)

First, you tear off the top of the brioche, a little knob on the top of the roll. Then you spoon some granita on the knob and pop it into your mouth. It's almost like a Sicilian slush sandwich.

After that first bite, you simply tear off piece of the remaining brioche, and scoop equal parts of granita on top.

I usually buy the newspaper "La Sicilia" and with my dictionary at hand, I try to muddle my way thru the paper. Sipping cappuccino, nibbling on that brioche and granite and reading that paper. I never want breakfast to end, to tell you the truth.

It is my time. My personal time that I treasure and cannot be replicated back home.

This afternoon, I thought about getting ready to go back home. There is a mountain of urgent things that I need to attend to right away, and I dread that flight home.

I call it "Pre-Partum Depression". Shrinks call it the "Stendhal Syndrome," the feeling that a visitor to a foreign country has before he leaves, never wanting to leave.

Except, I am not a foreigner. As an Italian citizen, I am classified by the Italian Government as a Citizen Living Abroad. I vote and everything.

Tomorrow will be my last post for this trip. I will return here for August and make ready for that trip. Three weeks here cost me less than $700 and the only reason it cost that much is that I ate dinner out five times, something I never do.

However, many of you reading my stuff suggested that I should write a book on Sicily. Actually, I HAVE written one. When I get home, I will put it together and probably self publish it. I want to match a humorous photo with each humorous piece that I have written, and I may do the photography when I return in August.

In any case, now I have to clean the fridge, wash the clothes (again), mop the floors, pack and get ready for my trip home. Pre-Partum Depression. (Sigh......).

3. Same Old Thing

Yesterday morning I (sadly) closed up the new place.

The last time I flew home in November, I told you that Alitalia was terrible.

This time I flew Northwest. Much better.

Ya, right.

First off, the Rome-Amsterdam connection was late, which means that I had to sprint through the Amsterdam airport (Schipol, my favorite airport) to catch the Amsterdam-Boston flight. I made it. My bags, of course, didn't.

Allegedly, they will be delivered tonight. Ya, right. Lost in Space, I fear.

I am worried about the economy though. On my return, Olga told me that business at the store has nose-dived despite the sale we had. Looks like we have our work cut out for us. We will have another huge sale and see if that helps, plus we have a lot of events planned, so hopefully the drop off is just an after Christmas thing. I sent all the photos of the condo that I took to Christine, who will post them on the website in a few days.

If you can't wait, send me an email (alfredzappala@yahoo.com) and I will send you some.

Well, back to the coal mines, I guess. By the way, I return to La Sicilia in May. Yay

4. Big News!

Big news today!

My son Matt emailed me and told me that he and his wife Lindsay are expecting their second child!

What wonderful news. I thank God always for all His blessings, and Matt and Lindz are the best parents ever. I am so happy for them. Now, I hope they finally name the kid Little Al or something like that! HAHA!

To celebrate, I went to Salvo's restaurant the Heritage in Acicatena. Salvo and his family run this wonderful little rustic restaurant where everything is homemade. It's like eating in your mom's house, the food is so good.

He promised to make me tonight "stocco" that fabled Sicilian fish stew that takes hours to make. When that stew is made in a normal house, it stinks the place up. It takes hours to prepare and gives off a "rich" cooking odor to be sure.

The dish is prepared with tomatoes, salted cod, black olives, potato, and a variety of herbs and spices.

My grandmother used to make it over the Christmas holidays and is considered to be one of the seven fished of Christmas here in this part of Sicily.

When he served it, I savored every bite knowing full well that this was my annual meal of this stew.

Boy, was it great!

I decided after eating this feast to drop by the Pardiso dell' Etna, a beautiful hotel in San Giovanni la Punta for a nightcap. This hotel is a small treasure. It was built in the 19th century by a Spanish prince as his summer home and filled with the most beautiful frescoes, and artwork.

In the summertime, every Sunday night there is an elegant disco on the grounds and people come from miles around dressed as if they were going to a fashion show, to dance to the pulsating music.

Tonight, a beautiful fireplace with a roaring fire greeted me. In a side room, a lovely gal was celebrating her eighteenth birthday with a big bash. All the teenagers were dressed to the nines and having a great time. Poor dad! He must have paid a small fortune for that party!

I enjoyed watching the teens dance as I drank my "Amaro Averna," that bitter Sicilian after dinner aperitif and thought to myself that this way a perfect ending to a wonderful day.

Tomorrow, I start to think about Tuesday's return to America. Business in America is terrible, and I have to figure out how to make sure that All things Sicilian has at least a respectable Christmas selling season. I came to Sicily to rest up a bit and to come up with a plan of attack, and now I am ready to return home and give it that old college try.

Still, receiving that wonderful news from Matt made everything else I did today a bonus.

Bravo, Matt and Lindz!

5. Going Home…or Leaving Home?

Today I am heading back to the U.S. after spending 7 weeks here in Sicily. (Sigh) Having lived here for a long stretch of time, I will miss the intangible happenings in the background of life. I will miss the church bell that sounds every morning at 7:00AM from the little church in Acicastello. I will miss the daily prayer (in Latin, the Hail Mary) that also is broadcast over the church's loudspeakers.

I will miss the sound of barking dogs and cows in the nearby farm.

I will miss the quiet of early morning as I water my beloved orange, lemon, olive and bergamot trees. Gosh they grew this year!

I will miss the sweet smell that fills my nostrils every day as I enter the panificio, the bread maker to pick up my bread.

I will miss the taste and texture of the food naturally organic and fresh.

I will miss watching Sicilian television at night, getting filled in on the news events here in Sicily and Italy.

I will even miss American movies that are dubbed in Italian and everything is out of sync.

I will miss driving like a banshee on the highways. I am getting the hang of it. I use my horn more than my brake now.

I will miss the splendor of Taormina, the majesty of Etna, the stark *Autostrada* ride to Palermo, the azure waters of Sciacca, the solitude of every hillside town from here to there.

I will miss everyday life here: shopping at the market, bagging my own groceries, getting a delicious "pollo al brace"(roasted chicken) fresh once a week.

I will miss dinner every Saturday night at Massimo's and Anna's house and the unbelievable food that Anna cooks. I will miss little Marzio, their 30 month old son calling me "zio Alfio".

I will miss hanging clothes on a clothes line, bringing my garbage to the garbage bin 100 yards away, washing the tiled floor, even changing the bed linens is different.

I will miss coffee at Urna, pizza at Heritage, going to the beach at Sant'Alessio di Sicilia. The public swimming pool at Madonna di Oliva in Viagrande where I have to wear a bathing cap if I want to swim.

Most of all though I will miss the people.

It will take me most of September to process my loss. I am sure that I will recover. I have lectures to prepare for the law schools where I teach, Sicilian business to attend, and a grand kids to gloat over.

My genes (and I suspect many of your genes) are home in Sicily, something that words cannot properly describe.

I will return again after Christmas, for the New Year.

Until then, in my heart, I will re-live daily life here, and wait for my next return to *La Bella Sicilia*: my home.

Chapter Thirty Three

Saint Agatha, Patron of Catania

Last year at this time I was in Sicily with Massimo. Today I am in front of my computer with a yard full of snow. What a difference a year makes! Last year I traveled to Sicily to witness (again) the Feast of Saint Agatha in Catania with its week long celebration February 1-6.

Agatha was a teenage girl who was martyred for her faith. Her father had chosen a wealthy businessman to be her husband—a marriage of convenience.—and Agatha refused to marry him telling her father that she wanted to devote herself to Jesus. After repeated advances by the businessman whom she rebuffed, she was killed by him, including having her breasts cut off. Thousands of miracles have been attributed to Saint Agatha over the centuries and now her feast week is one of Italy's biggest celebrations.

In honor of the saint a popular Sicilian treat is eaten during this time, a small cake covered with a delicious pistachio frosting with a cherry on top: *li minuzzi di Sant'Agata*, the breast of Saint Agatha. It is served everywhere! Next to the July Feast of Saint Rosalie in Palermo, this is Sicily's biggest event.

As Massimo, Anna and I approached the festivities a sea of humanity surrounded us. Feeling a little uncomfortable with all the people, I sought out a vantage point to enjoy the festivities comfortably. Discovering a great place close to the main area of the city's downtown, I watched the hundreds of boys and men dressed in white robes processing to the Duomo as they pulled the wagon (*vara*) upon which the statue of Saint Agatha was displayed. Each rope that was attached to the front and back of the *vara* was at least 200 yards long and the hundreds of the devotees were pulling the cart very slowly. Thousands of the faithful surrounded the *vara* each holding in his or her hand a three foot long candle which was given to the men for the vara as a symbol of their love for Saint Agatha.

Behind the *vara* a truck carried the overflow candles! It was a magnificent sight!

Later that evening, we visited a cloistered convent nearby (a convent where the nuns have taken the vow of silence). Once a year, the nuns appear on the convent's balcony dressed in white and sing the Ave Maria. It is a centuries-old tradition. While these angels sang, tens of thousands silently observed. It was so quiet you could hear a pin drop. I got a lump in my throat and silently thanked God for giving me an opportunity to witness such a holy sight. As soon as the nuns completed the hymn, they disappeared back into the convent for another year.

As we returned home, I mentioned to Massimo that I wanted to try a Big Mac at the only McDonald's in Catania.

"Alfred" Massimo said, "You are crazy."

Anyway, we proceeded into McDonald's and for the first time in his life, Massimo and Anna ate a Big Mac and fries, a Sicilian Big Mac and fries. In no way were the tastes even remotely connected to the US version. As a matter of fact, I gagged.

Here we were in the culinary capital of the world eating big Macs.

"Not bad, Alfred," Massimo said trying to make me feel better as we searched for an antacid, "but of course I will kill you if we ever go there again! Let's go eat some pasta now!"

Chapter Thirty-Four

Going Native

1. Native in Two Days

Two months ago I mentioned to our design manager Christine that Massimo and I were planning to attend the Cibus International Food Show being held in the northern city of Parma the beginning of May.

She suggested that as the person in charge of both store and Internet visual presentation that perhaps the experience would be invaluable to her if she were to accompany us. Since she had never been to Sicily (she had designed all the stores to replicate Sicily based solely on my photos and verbal descriptions) and is Irish in background to boot, I decided that if we wanted to present Sicily accurately that maybe she should tag along.

As a trained artist from the School of the Museum of Fine Arts, Boston I concluded that the trip would stimulate her creative side. Planning to stay in Sicily only two days after the show, then to Via Grande, Chris marveled at the colors of the landscape and the texture of the land. Wide-eyed, she gobbled down her first Sicilian breakfast.

After breakfast we traveled the back roads of Pedara and Nicolosi examining the vegetation and spring flowers along the way. An explosion of colors in these mountain villages announced that springtime was in full bloom. We jumped on the *autostrada* and headed north to Taormina. Usually I park my car down in the beach area of Taormina (Taormina Mare) area and head into Taormina on the tram (the Funivia) in order to avoid traffic. We enjoyed the short tram ride and by this time Chris was on her third roll of film capturing image after image of the sweeping horizon as we approached this ancient town.

I once spent 14 days exploring Taormina's nooks and crannies, but over a three hour period I did what I could to show her the best of the best. Corso Umberto (the main walking promenade) was thronged with sightseers and the shops were bristling with activity. Chris snapped away gathering hundreds of display ideas. She flipped at the floral displays that hung from each apartment atop the promenade. We visited the ancient churches, spent a couple of hours wandering up and down my favorite streets and browsed the shops. The brilliant, shining Sicilian sun welcomed us. No visit to Taormina is complete without a quick cup of espresso and a *gelato* at the Wunderbar overlooking perhaps the finest vista of Naxos Bay. Troubadours serenaded us as we sipped our coffee. After a quick pizza at my favorite ristorante, we jumped on the tram and headed to Giardini Naxos, Sicily's first settlement.

This ancient town is a wonder all to itself and friends that I know come to Sicily only to visit this place, yet in the three short hours that we were there, Chris was exposed to Naxos' beauty. Funny, right about then I detected that this little Irish gal was beginning to understand the allure and majesty of my Island. A short trip to Isola Bella, and one glimpse of the most photographed swimming spot in Europe sealed it for Chris. In 6 short hours she had gone completely native. When I dropped her off, Massimo swore he heard her talking to herself that she had a new found respect for the lava vases that we sell. Massimo and I laughed; surrounded as she was by the beauty of Etna she thought only about lava vases! In truth, she was speechless for the first time in her life!

Finally we left and headed down the mountain toward Trecastagni, the real reason for the two day diversion to Sicily to attend the Feast of Sant'Alfio there, as countless of my forefathers had. This has been my yearly pilgrimage for seven straight years and Chris was going to see her first Sicilian religious festival. Upon arriving, we walked the streets of the town visiting the Church of Sant'Alfio and the Hall of Miracles and proceeded down the festival streets enjoying the sights and sounds of various hawking vendors. I spotted a gorgeous Moroccan rug that a street vendor was selling and after 15 minutes of haggling bought it for the villa. Chris picked up souvenirs for her kids. Massimo did the same for his wife. At dusk, we witnessed the finest fireworks display imaginable and we caught it all on video too! Eating at my favorite caffè (bar) at Plaza Marconi, we devoured "scacciata", both the famous spinach and cheese and the meat version and sipped local wine.

Tired from our busy two day whirlwind tour, Chris snoozed in the car on the way back home. I remarked to Massimo, "Think she enjoyed herself?" The glow on her sleeping face answered the question. She now understood our Island. Chris had gone native in record time.

2. Sicilian Doubting Thomas

It was quite an accomplishment earlier this month when Massimo, Christine and I traveled to New York City for the Fancy Food Show.

The Fancy Food Show, held every year at the Jacob Javits Center by the National Association for the Specialty Food Trade, is the biggest event in the gourmet food business, more than 25,000 owners of shops and markets attend this important event to view new products for possible sale at their stores from more than 2,200 companies world-wide who display their newest products.

The Fancy Food Show also has an annual award competition at that time and gives out awards in twenty different categories. These awards are the equivalent of the Oscar of the food business, so in every sense, the Fancy Food Show is the "Premier Event" of the food industry.

Early in June, our Christine Leone approached me and suggested that we enter our Valle dell'Etna Pistacchio Nut Cream into the competition. "Forget it, Christine," I said," We'll never have a chance. All the big companies who spend hundreds of thousands of dollars in marketing and advertising have entered products. We'll never stand a chance." She persisted in her quest to enter the nut cream in the competition and after a couple of weeks of driving me crazy, I relented and gave her the ok. She was giving me a headache and I figured that would quiet her down a bit.

Chris prepared the samples and submitted the products. The 98 Finalists and then twenty Winners were chosen by close to 100 specialty food retailers from around the country. The competition began in June when NASFT member companies submitted nearly 1,600 entries totaling more than 3,500 products in hopes of winning the specialty food industry's most prestigious honor, according to the NASFT. To our shock and amazement, we were notified that our product had made the cut and was a Finalist!

"Don't get excited, Chris," I said. "You did a great job getting us this far, but I don't want you to be disappointed when we lose." I was preparing her to accept disappointment, as I was sure that one of the "biggies" would surely win.

We set up our booth at the show and this year a delegation of Italian vendors were there from Milan, Venice, Florence, even Sicily. They came over to our booth one by one and wished us well. "Alfred," one of them said to me, "No Sicilian has ever won such an award in this competition other than in olive oil, so don't get your hopes up."

"It would be wonderful if you somehow did win," he said. "Sicily has an unemployment rate of 22% and this would be wonderful for manufacturers, as it would give them courage to market their wonderful products in America, but really Alfred, you don't stand a chance."

The evening of the second day of the three-day show, Chris and I went to the awards dinner.

Like the Oscars, they had the press there, entertainment, all the trappings of a major event. The host asked all the finalists to sit in chairs on the stage. Chris, who started this project, represented our tiny company. She was sitting on the enormous stage, surrounded by many big companies. In fact, I bet we were the tinest one there!

One by one the finalists were announced and a picture was flashed on the enormous screen behind the screen: four finalists per category. I was sitting in the audience, amazed at the intensity of the crowd, as there were nearly 1,000 in attendance.

Our category was finally announced.

"And the winner in the category of Outstanding Jam, Preserve or spread is Valle dell'Etna Nut Cream from All Things Sicilian!"

Shocked, I looked at Christine as she bounded to the podium to accept the award: a trophy just like the Oscar!

I was shocked, and so were all the giant companies! All the next day at the show, we were visited by company presidents, purchasing managers, distributors and agents, asking about the product. More than 250 different companies visited our booth to wish us well, congratulate us or inquire about selling the product themselves. One by one the Italian companies came. The look of pride that they had in their eyes said it all.

"Alfred," one of them said, "Your company did a very good thing for Italy and Sicily today, grazie tante." For me, that statement was our reward. For our tiny company to get recognition for our beloved Island. Well, what more can I ask?

As you are reading this I am back in Sicily with Massimo scouring Sicily for more products. We are traveling to Ragusa, Palermo, Marsala and tiny hamlets here and there. We now have a story to tell!

Chapter Thirty-Five

Perfection

I ate the perfect meal last night. I mean it. That once in a decade meal that you think about for months afterwards. I went to Piccolo Mondo in Viagrande, my friend Carmelo's place. I have been going there for years. However, last night was an unforgettable repast that goes in my Hall of Fame list of "Things To Drool Over in My Mind While Stuck in Traffic in Boston" list that I have kept for years.

Carmelo told me that his friend had dropped him off a basket of mushrooms that had just been picked from nearby Zafferana, known far and wide for its mushrooms. Do I want some? Dumb question. Of course I said yes.

He drizzled the mushrooms with a little oil and lightly salted them. He had cut them in slices about a quarter inch thick and three inches in diameter. Then he grilled them. Instead of those tacky things that I buy in any American market, these things literally melted in my mouth and the flavor sent me to heaven.

That was the appetizer. Next he grilled me some "agnello," lamb chops from a nearby farm. Each morsel of these grilled gems exploded with flavor in my mouth, and I picked every morsel off the bones which were so brittle you could practically eat them too.

As a throw in, he made us some eggplant with tomato, cheese, pignoli, raisins and swordfish, topped with a balsamic reduction. Fresh spinach and salad as a side. Bread that was still piping hot. Truly a meal of epic proportions.

As I never eat dessert while here (If I ate dessert at every meal, I'd be 300 pounds in no time), I asked for fruit instead. He brought over strawberries, peaches, cantaloupe, apricots, mountain berries and oranges with the stems on that all were hanging on the trees hours earlier. Each was better than the other. A nice carafe of "vino rosso di casa" complimented this meal of perfection. Cost of this meal including a tip: 30 euros (about $36.00). Truly, I was a happy camper.

BTW: Carmelo and I talked a little business. Home prices are dropping quickly. Like the USA, no one can get a loan. New jobs are few and far between. The euro (which is good news for us) is rapidly losing its value due to the plight of Greece, Spain and Portugal. This guy, who is a Sicilian rock, is getting worried. Last night, about 20 people were in the place while I was there. The temp was in the high

60s yesterday and a bit windy. Tomorrow, I have to wash the car because I parked it under a tree last night and it dropped all sorts of stuff everywhere. My wipers left a green muck on the windshield when I tried to wash it. No wonder no one parked on that side of the street. I should know better.

Today I will mooch a dinner from Massimo to cost average my food. I will spend zero today to eat a great meal that his wife Anna will make. However, I will bring the dessert (cannoli) and maybe I will eat one too!

Chapter Thirty-Six

The Mighty Green Thumb

Only a complete idiot cannot grow things in Sicily.

The soil, the climate, the sun all have contributed to plentiful harvest and bountiful land for thousands of years.

Since all my neighbors have beautiful plants, trees, flowers, vegetation on their decks, I figured, why not me?

I had two big flower boxes on the front and back of the condo, and wanting to be a good neighbor, I figured that I would go to the local "Piano Fiore" (greenhouse) to get a few things and plant them in the boxes.

Gotta keep up appearance, you know.

So off I went.

At the greenhouse, I talked to my friend who I had done business with before.

I explained to him that there are long stretches when I am not here, and that I needed something that needed little water.

"You need something that gets its moisture from the air" he said.

"Sì," said I.

He pointed to a bunch of cacti he had. (That's plural for cactus according to my Italian spell check)

"This will do it," he said.

Buying cactus wasn't exactly what I had in mind, but what the heck. I bought 8 cacti.

Anyway, back to the house I went, and before you know it, I had them all planted in the two boxes.

"Hmm..." I said.

"Looks like Arizona," I thought.

Off I went back to my friend.

"There's gotta be something else," I said to my friend.

"Alfred, plants need water. Even you know that," he said. "Here, try these!"

I bought a couple of these beautiful red and purple bush-type plants and planted them next to the cacti

I then knocked on the door of my next door neighbor, Mrs. Longo, and asked her if she would water the plants when I returned to America.

She said, "Sure!"

Last year I asked Massimo to water my plants and they all died, so I wasn't taking any chances.

Mrs. Longo has a forest on her deck, so what's a few more to mind?

Anyway, the cacti look great, and when you come here to visit, you will experience the great "Giardino di Alfred," kinda like Bush Gardens was, 100 years ago!

Chapter Thirty-Seven

Tripping the Light Fantastic

I decided to do some "social research" and visit the most famous disco in Sicily: the fabulous outdoor disco called "Mantica" in Acitrezza, home of the beautiful people and me.

Being from Lawrence and knowing a thing or two about social haunts from all over the world, I figured I see what all the commotion was about this place. I had heard a million times that this was THE place to go.

Since it is located right at the bottom of the hill where I live, I said to myself "Al, America is curious".

So off I went.

Dressed in my usual casual-elegant garb (Eddie Baeur black dungarees, a black shirt untucked, a sports coat that fit like a glove and loafers, along with a little cologne thrown on for good measure, I headed to the disco, purely for research, that is.

La Mantica resembles one of those Havana night cubs that you saw in the *Godfather*.

Outdoors, palms trees, exotic plants everywhere, elegant fixtures, stunning indirect lighting, fancy drinks with umbrellas and fruit in them, pulsating music: the works.

The crowd was an older one too from 30 to 60 I'd say.

I never saw a room full of Sophia Loren's and Marcello Mastroiannis until tonight though.

Wow.

The women were so beautiful I thought I should pay for the view and kept throwing dollar bills at them, and the men: all movie star quality, dressed in hand-made suits, beautiful shirts ties and shoes.

And of course me, dressed in my usual Eddie Baeur garb.

Talk about being vastly underdressed.

The place opened at 1:00 AM. Yes, that's right. 1:00 AM. Wayyyy past my bedtime.

I got there at 12:45 and stood in line, a long line and paid my 15 euros entrance fee.

The music was throbbing. Kinda like a cross between salsa and Caribbean music.

Within ten minutes, the dance floor was mobbed.

However, the way they dance is very unusual. People do not flail away the way we do in America. It seemed that people were moving to the music, swaying to the music, while engaging in deep conversation. The dancing, it seemed, was secondary to the conversation.

It looked to me that it was more important to be seen by others than to enjoy who you were with.

It looked like they lifted their feet a little, but talking was more important than dancing.

Thus, the first thing I learned tonight was conversation was the most important thing, not the style of dance.

Honestly, America has much better dancers. Being from Lawrence and having been to many a joint with beautiful Latina ladies dancing away, I'd say that "we" dance way better than "they" do.

Just a general observation.

By 2:30 AM, I was so tired that I forgot why I was there. I was so bushed that even if the real Sophia Loren came up to me, I would have taken a rain check I think.

Striking up a conversation with several of the females there I also noticed a couple of interesting things: This particular cut of women is just as "plastic" as the disco queens in America. While they looked elegant, most were as deep as a puddle. I imagine the same is true for the men.

My observation is that discos are important, but not to me. If I were younger, a lot younger, and "on the hunt "so to speak, then I'd be in my glory. However, I am not and the conclusion is this: visit a disco once, but for old fogies like me, a nice piano bar, a beach, a nice restaurant, a museum, even a home party with friends is a much more pleasant way to spend an evening.

Plus, you can get to bed at a decent hour, for heaven's sake.

By the way, floral prints are in this summer for women. I saw a lot of frilly things tonite. Plus way too much perfume.

One last point: I told you in a piece a few articles back about the electric gate that is broken in my condo. I had to climb over the damn thing a couple nights ago. The administrator of the condo told me that it would be a few more days until the part came in, and basically said tough luck until then. I asked him if I could look at it and maybe fix it myself. He said, "Sure!"

This afternoon I swung by the hardware store and bought 4 feet of chain and a lock. I chained the damn thing open- and I have the only key.

American ingenuity. I chuckled all night thinking about the expression on his face when he sees the chain.

He"d better get a bolt cutter, as I "lost" the key!

Never, ever, mess with someone from Lawrence.

Especially a Sicilian from Lawrence!

Chapter Thirty-Eight

Mom

A True Story

I attended the Holy Rosary School in Lawrence, Massachusetts from grades 1 to 3. I never "adapted" to the nuns and they never adapted to me.

"Conduct" was always an issue to them. It didn't matter that in those days breakfast was a cup of coffee that you dunked your toast in. It didn't matter in those days that a nine year old kid had caffeine high by eight o'clock in the morning. In those days, that is what a kid had for breakfast.

Coffee for kids was the norm.

Anyway, I was a rambunctious kid and the nuns basically hated me.

My mom was a bull dozer in those days. She was thirty-nine years old and a real work horse.

When I gave her a hard time, a good swat was swiftly administered, but the nuns chose to administer a little psychological punishment in addition to the corporal punishment by either sending a note home or requesting a meeting. The nuns knew the ramifications of notifying my mom. That meant a meeting.

That dreaded meeting.

Upon opening the note that I dutifully had to carry home from the nuns, Sister Catherine Angela in particular was a prolific note-writer, mom would administer a pre-emptive thrashing to me: kinda like she was loosening up before the big game and then grab her coat, me and we'd head over to the convent.

The convent.

Where God lived.

That dark, silent place where holy people lived.

Nuns.

What chance did a little kid have, for heaven's sake? Me against God? Forget it. No chance.

Standing there as good old Sister Catherine Angela informed mom about my behavior, none of it good, a gnawing feeling gripped my already hysterical stomach.

The walk home was particularly brutal. Squeezing my arm like a vise, I knew she wasn't a happy camper.

However, I found an unsuspecting ally in mom. "That nun is an idiot!" she'd say, "But you are a bigger idiot for getting in trouble."

To make a long story short, the day the next report card came in was my last day at Holy Rosary.

I had gotten an "F" in conduct. Not only an "F," but a red "F".

Only the worst of the worst got red Fs. Future criminals, thugs and Liberals. Those type of people.

I remember vividly that day as she opened up the envelope, saw the red "F", and then committed the biggest sacrilege ever: she ripped the report card in half!

Oh my God. I was going to hell. I was going to burn worse that Satan.

My mom intentionally and with malice aforethought, destroyed Church property. In no time the Cardinal and maybe even the Pope would hear about this. I would be ex-communicated for sure. I don't care how many candy bars my mom had to sell for the nuns, I was still screwed.

Ripping a report card trumps candy bars, everyone knows that.

Horrified, I gasped as mom grabbed my arm. Back to the sacred convent we went.

Sister Catherine Angela met us at the door and then mom finished her act of heresy: she took out the report card, ripped it into TINY pieces, and threw it in her face.

I suspected that something out of the ordinary was taking place. This didn't seem to be the normal mom-Sister Catherine Angela meeting with subsequent thrashing that I was accustomed to.

No, this was better. Much better. Kinda like in its own category better. One for the Ages, I thought.

"He's out" mom said. "I am sending him to Sacred Heart."

Sacred Heart.

Hell. The Sing Sing for problem kids. Sacred Heart School for Boys in Andover, Massachusetts. Renowned far and wide as a school for "problem" boys.

Run by The Brothers of the Sacred Heart, a misnomer if there ever was one. Young kids who wore black robes and kicked the crap out of you for looking at them. The Green Berets of Catholicism.

Renowned for its academics, they guaranteed success for your youngster, one way or the other. "If nothing else, your son will be literate, polite, and know how to study when we get through with him," the Principal named "Brother Director" promised mom.

Truer words were never spoken. Knowledge administered with the back of the hand, the front of the hand, hockey sticks, you name it.

For five long years I sat at that desk with hands folded, heels of the shoes touching, and if I opened my mouth even a smidgen, they would close it for me.

Learning Gestapo style.

Any way, I ended up doing five years hard labor at Sacred Heart. Attending class six days a week. We received a WEEKLY report card.

Yup, the old kid here spent time in the Guantanamo of the Church.

My friends there would ask me why I was there. Some of these guys were real tough.

Fighting, playing hooky from school, stealing, you name it.

However, they all used to gasp when I told them:

"Mom ripped up my report card with the red 'F' on it and threw it at the nun".

In many ways, that story made my reputation at Sacred Heart.

From then on, it was straight up.

Thanks, Mom!

Post script: My mom passed away in September 2009 at the young age of ninety. She was surrounded by a loving family of three children, seven grandchildren, and five great-grandchildren.

On one of her last days, I remember reading her this story. She loved it. "Alfred", she said, "That nun was nuts, but the best thing I ever did was send you to Sacred Heart."

True, so true.

Marquis Book Printing Inc.

Québec, Canada
2010